Absalom Hazlett

Absalom Hazlett

A Loyal Soldier in John Brown's Army

Spencer Sadler

America Through Time®
ADDING COLOR TO AMERICAN HISTORY

America Through Time is an imprint of Fonthill Media LLC
www.through-timae.com
office@through-time.com

Published by Arcadia Publishing by arrangement with Fonthill Media LLC
For all general information, please contact Arcadia Publishing:
Telephone: 843-853-2070
Fax: 843-853-0044
E-mail: sales@arcadiapublishing.com
For customer service and orders:
Toll-Free 1-888-313-2665

www.arcadiapublishing.com

First published 2020

ISBN 978-1-63499-279-4

Typeset in Sabon 10.5pt on 13.5pt
Printed and bound in England

Acknowledgments

It takes the cooperation of everyone around an author to complete a book. A writing project such as this takes teamwork and people understanding that a writer needs time to write, people going out of their way to chip in to help provide research materials, people giving permission to use pictures, and people showing interest, providing support, and offering kind words of encouragement.

Tim Noakes at Stanford University Special Collections graciously and quickly provided a folder that held important keys to the story. Getting this folder early in the process gave me hope in the feasibility of the project. Harry Hunt has a Flickr account to feature his photography work. He attended the Absalom "Albert" Hazlett State Historical Marker Dedication and took a collection of photos that he posted and gave permission for me to use. Dawn Gardner and Sprigg Lynn gave permission to use the photos from the Kennedy Farm Facebook page. Dawn, Sprigg, and his father, South Lynn, are committed to preserving and sharing American history, which is evident in their tireless work in restoring and running Kennedy Farm. Ann Hull is the Director at the Franklin County Historical Society and quickly signed off on photos of the Ritner House.

I have people that I worked with who were encouraging and covered for me when I needed time to write. I coached JV football with Malcolm Lewis, and there were many times he attempted to send me home motivating me to write. Curtis Jones was also a coach that wanted to help free time up for me to make progress on the book. Joe Taylor was there to talk about the book and listen to some of my ideas before I put them onto the page. Once they were on the page, Peter Lockovich pitched in to help read the manuscript and offer suggestions.

Sincere thanks go to the publishing team and all here in America and in England who helped make the book the best that it could be.

My family was extremely supportive of this endeavor. My wife, Stephanie, who probably knows me better than I know myself, knows that I am a slow, methodical writer who is easily distracted, so she kept the house quiet and her bathroom breaks and laundry loads at a minimum while I was at home writing. I owe so much of what is good in my life to her. My sons, Morgan and Malcolm, helped keep me on pace by checking in with me daily and cheering on my increasing word count. Last but not least, of course, there are my supportive parents, Clarence and Marion, who have been great providers for me and my family, and they were also great teachers of an enduring, life-long work ethic that I pray that my sons will emulate.

Contents

Introduction

At times, this creative nonfiction book may read like an action/adventure story. At times, it will seem like a courtroom drama. Yet, overall, it is a classic hero's quest story—a story of a young man rebelling against the overwhelming institution of slavery.

The premise of this story is quite simple, and it is one that has been told over and over again in American cinema. A group of thieves attempt to pull off a grand heist, which seems pretty simple at face value. That is until we start asking the basic questions of conflict, motivation, and story structure.

For example, who are these anti-heroes attempting this heist, and from whose perspective will the story be told? Where is the setting, and is it significant? What is the group stealing and why? Structurally, how will the story be told?

Once we begin answering the questions to John Brown's raid at Harpers Ferry and peeling back the layers, the story can become very complex in theme and mechanics. This is a story eight years in the making, for it was abandoned numerous times because of how difficult the story was to harness in a traditional manner. One stumbling block was the impulse to romanticize the raiders. Instead, it was found that the best presentation is to raise the all-embracing theme and then leave it alone. The most complex thematic rhetorical question in the story—is it okay to break the law if the law violates one's religious or moral convictions? It also offers structural complexity in asking how all of these multitudinous parts will be held together to make a cohesive story.

To answer these questions, the story is told in an unorthodox manner—through a minor character, Absalom "Albert" Hazlett—to simplify the story and help limit the focus. John Brown was the architect of the raid, but it touched the lives of many. Also, one might find the shape of the story quite quirky because the story's structure is in reverse chronological order to meet the demands placed on the story and its multiple moving parts.

Narratives that encompass twenty-two characters can pose problems when put into a straight, linear story. One catch-all method used is that some events are returned to in the text to help orient the reader and to fill in contextual gaps, signifying that other actions are happening simultaneously around that singular event. One example is when the plan is falling apart at Harpers Ferry: Hazlett saves himself, hides out in the bushes to escape in the cliffs, and then eventually returns to the Arsenal building overlooking John Brown's Fort. In the meantime, Osborne Anderson is on a mission to recruit and arm slaves. He then ultimately makes his way back to meeting Hazlett at the Arsenal building, so the time spent at the Arsenal building becomes a home base to not only the two characters but to the reader, as well. Another such event is when the two find a rowboat to cross the Potomac to begin their journey to the Kennedy Farmhouse. Multiple events with many characters surround that development, so we return to that rowboat as a pivotal event.

Though this is a historical work of nonfiction, the intention is to make it more of a narrative. To do that requires this rationale, outlined in John Truby's *The Anatomy of Story*:

> The designing principle is what organizes the story as a whole. It is the internal logic of the story, what makes the parts hang together organically so that the story becomes greater than its parts. It is what makes the story original.

Much has been written on John Brown and the raid at Harpers Ferry. There are volumes of newspaper and magazine articles, books on his life and his contemporaries, websites, historical court documents, congressional transcripts, and surviving personal letters. Yet, the originality of this story is not only in what Truby calls "the designing principle" of the story's structure but in the perspective of a subordinate character thrust into historical importance.

By structuring a story through Hazlett's experiences, we can see how this event had a ripple effect that impacted the lives of many. Also, by structuring the story in this fashion, we realize our protagonist's historical significance before we see how his everyday life played out and inspired prominence. By already knowing the outcome of the story, we can trace that to the fatal climactic scene that ultimately triggered his destiny, meeting America's most notorious homegrown terrorist, John Brown.

The traditional plot diagram is not sacrificed for the structure. Instead, the introductions are made up of the posthumous dedications. The inciting incident is the trial that led to Hazlett being hanged. The rising action is the raid, and the climax is Hazlett meeting John Brown for the first time. The dénouement is Hazlett at home in Indiana.

Also, about the story's backward narrative, it is not a direct, straight line hurtling us directly into the past. Instead, we go into the past to work our way to the present of the narrative, from a past date up to a current date that might even require a flashback for explanation. Ultimately, the isolated incidents will link the chapters together and make the story bind together into a cohesive narrative. At times then, there will be some overlap to tie the narrative together. This will probably make more sense in the practical reading of the book against this theoretical explanation. In all, the story was intended to feel like it is always moving forward, answering the driving question "and then what happens?"

Finally, the other major component of this story is the dialog; the intention was to keep it as historically accurate as possible. If a quote is endnoted, that either signifies that statement was lifted directly from a source citing the quote from some sort of eyewitness account, text, newspaper, transcript, or it is a dramatized statement of fact from a credible source. Other uncited dialogue was created or hoisted from history for the basic mechanics of story, moving the conflict forward, revealing character or illuminating the background information or subtext of a scene, but all dialogue has a historical basis and context.

1

A Road Sign Dedication

A Devotion to Freedom (March 27, 2009)

The Pennsylvania Historical and Museum Commission put a marker along the road outside of the college town of Indiana, Pennsylvania, commemorating the birthplace and boyhood farm of a man who gave his life for a fundamental belief in freedom. Local organizations gathered together a ceremony for the unveiling.

Two gentlemen in proper, mid-nineteenth-century attire were there to uncover a road sign that reads in state's colors—blue and gold:

> A staunch abolitionist, Hazlett became a lieutenant in John Brown's provisional army and participated in the raid on Harpers Ferry Arsenal in 1859. He was captured, tried, convicted, and hanged for his involvement following the failed Harpers Ferry attack. This incident, intended to arm slaves to fight for their own freedom, was a major catalyst for the outbreak of the Civil War. Hazlett was born and raised near here.

Right on the outskirts of town, Route 954 shoots over to 56, a pre-Revolution Native American trail that connected trading posts all the way from present-day Johnstown to the forks of Fort Pitt, where the three rivers meet in what is now known as "The Point" in downtown Pittsburgh. The sign sits along the hilly twists and turns of Indiana's 6th Street extension, where the Hazlett family once owned and worked a large chunk of land.

The terrain ranges from gently rolling hills to jutted outcrops, yet with some planning and work, it could be scalped for fertile topsoil and cultivated into a productive farm. Large farms require large families, and Alexander and Sarah Hazlett produced many helping hands—nine boys and two girls. They had no idea that their sixth child born on September

21, 1837—Absalom—would be a crusader and carve a searing niche into American history.

Heading east, farms that have been in operation for generations are proof that farming is in the blood, especially when tilling this kind of landscape on the foothills of the Allegheny Mountains, but today on those farms, gas wells have been posted up in the middle of those crops. Looking like metal aliens with thin arms plopped in the middle of a cornfield, the wells sit as emblems of some sort of assurance, passed down to ensure future generations of family wealth. Farmers were able to cash in on the Marcellus shale boom of recent years, but the Hazlett farm left the hands of the family generations ago.

A gas company office and warehouse face the marker. Caddy-corner, across the highway, a Bar-B-Que joint, and a three-front strip mall sit. Beyond the sign on both sides, housing developments are back off the thoroughfare, showcasing mid-level homes for local, upper-middle-class company guys and Indiana University of Pennsylvania professors as well as much larger homes big enough for bank presidents and corporate CEOs.

There were about sixty adults and children at the ceremony to honor Albert, including some distant relatives, members of the local NAACP, a group of teachers and students from Ben Franklin Elementary School, the director and board members of the Indiana County Historical Society, state and township representatives from the transportation department and museum commission, and the organization dedicated to the local history of the Underground Railroad: the Blairsville Passport to Freedom Experience.

The end of March in Western Pennsylvania poses an ever-present threat of rain, so trying to schedule an event was tricky business. As luck would have it, however, it was sunny and clear, yet there was still a chill in the air that kept the guys mimicking the era in their wool coats from being overdressed and hot. The elementary school kids seemed comfortable in windbreakers and hoodies. They were happy to be out of school but also kind of bored. Most kids were really unsure as to the magnitude of the historical figure's significance that they were there to pay tribute to. They have talked about John Brown and the event that took place at Harpers Ferry in class, but it was just another event in the string of other events that needed to be memorized for the state's standardized test. The way they saw it, John Brown was a kooky old man with a big white beard and crazy eyes from the *Tragic Prelude* mural.

After some brief speeches and introductions about the dedication, the children's chorus sang "Lift Every Voice and Sing," which is oft referred to as the Black American National Anthem, written by James Weldon Johnson. Then came the moment that all had assembled for: the PHMC's cover was taken from the marker, unveiling the true reason why the man, Absalom "Albert" Hazlett, is so important to our great nation. "He was a martyr for freedom," one of the presenters said.

Yet he and his cohorts were hated at the time, explained another. They were seen as terrorists, killing for a misguided cause, yet to Hazlett and those other abolitionists who thought like him, brutality had to be used to eliminate brutality. The raids were ugly but necessary.

The local historian, Clarence Stephenson, was a tall, lanky man and as kind, soft-spoken, and gentle as Mr. Fred Rogers. Stephenson spent decades writing several volumes on Indiana history, taking the time to interview hundreds of local residents, trace family histories, and record their personal stories. In full detail, the volumes cover major events, businesses that came and went and those who owned them, county and town politics and the specific histories of political figures and races, and the overall growth of the town. Ever since he completed his last volume as an old and weary man, he seemed completely burned out on talking about Indiana County history. Whenever anyone began reminiscing about the days of old, or if he was asked questions about if he remembered this or that, or if he ever knew what happened to an ex-colleague, neighbor, or coworker, or if they would ask ancestry types of questions, or if he remembered an old county official, he would always reply, "Everything I know is in those books. If it wasn't in there, then, I didn't know about it. I wrote down and published everything I know about Indiana, so everything I know is in those books."

Now, at ninety, Stephenson's mind was still rather sharp, but he spoke slowly and deliberately. He had large feet and knobby knees that seemed to be up by his ears when he sat down, like Ichabod Crane from Disney's 1949 version of *The Legend of Sleepy Hollow*, and when he got up after they called him up to the table-top podium to speak, he rose deliberately and slowly. The podium sat on fold-up banquet tables in the parking lot of the restaurant, which was a small log cabin-veneered eatery named Pennsylvania Barbeque. Stephenson laboriously hoisted himself to his feet and steadied himself with his cane and began speaking.[1]

"Thank you for gathering here today," he said to begin to give his keynote presentation in his quiet and shaky voice:

> The story of Absalom "Albert" Hazlett starts out slowly and methodically down in Green Township around Devil's Elbow. Some vow this area is haunted because of the multiple car accidents that happened at the sharp bend.
>
> But Mr. Hazlett's story, that story, starts like many who grew up as farmers in the region. Then it shifts and changes drastically when he

> was about nineteen or twenty and he moved to Kansas to work on his brother's farm. It was there that he met like-minded individuals who believed deeply in the morality of killing in the name of biblical righteousness. When Kansas was about to turn into a slave state, Mr. Hazlett was spurred to action, and he was going to find a way to stop the spread of what he knew to be the scourge of our country.
>
> Assuredly, Albert, as he wanted his friends and family to refer to him, was an abolitionist long before meeting John Brown, but at twenty, he was impressionable. He wasn't old and jaded, like me, [he paused for laughter or some sort of reaction that never reached the fifth graders.] Albert's father, like John Brown's father, was deeply religious and lived a quiet life, but he taught all his children that it was sheer evil to own another human being. Yes, his family saw blacks as human beings. You children may not understand the implications of that, but this view divided our nation. Some did not see blacks as full human.

One of the kids laughed, whether out of nervousness, silliness, or the absurdity of the notion, and Mr. Stephenson paused before continuing. "Many whites at the time saw blacks as three-fifths of a person. Do you know what that means?" He peered into the wide-eyed faces of the fifth graders.

He scanned the tightknit crowd of kids, huddled together like little penguins against a sweeping blizzard. No one answered. They looked at each other and reacted in smirks and faces that clearly said, "I don't know, do you?"

Stephenson continued waiting patiently, caught a couple of confused faces, and waited a little longer until it was beginning to get uncomfortable and awkward even for the adults that stood looking on. He looked down at his notes, and then he looked back up and began to riff a bit.

> For almost a hundred years before the end of the Civil War, the United States legislated at the Constitutional Convention that slaves would account for three-fifths of a person. There were several reasons for this, but the main one was because when they counted up the people of an area for congressional apportionment, they could not count slaves as a real person because they couldn't own property, and, thus, would not need representation. So, during a census, the south could only count their slaves as three-fifths of a person and that would determine the number of seats given to that county. This was an agreed compromise for fairness between the northern and southern states that was ironed out at the Convention of 1787. It was intended to keep the large southern plantation owners from dominating congress.

> Well, seeing blacks as less-than-human was and still is deeply embedded into our society. Because we are a country built on slavery from the very beginning, it is almost baked right into American culture, sadly, even today.

He looked back down at his notes and got back on track. The children reacted with blank stares. This man was way older than their grandfathers.

> We're not really sure if Albert heard about John Brown when he was in Kansas, but in the early part of 1857, he went to Kansas and joined a volunteer Free State Military Company and told others about it when he came back to Indiana to visit. It was about that time when he was introduced to a radical and notable abolitionist named James Montgomery.
>
> We don't know what made Albert tick, just like we really don't know the personal thoughts of any human, yet there are some things about him we are sure of. First of all, he was no saint. The newspaper *The Johnstown Echo* alleged that Hazlett worked in the town as a canal boatman in his teens. He was accused of selling his employer's boat and team but returned the money when caught to avoid prosecution.[2] In addition, he was said to have hung out with a gang of horse thieves but turned State's evidence and testified against his confederates at their trial in Elmira, New York.[3]
>
> His brother, John, was an abolitionist and moved to Missouri, right over the border from Kansas, because of the stir and migration to fight to save Kansas from being a slave state. We also know from what has been passed down through the years that his brother John and he had political motivations. We know that a mutual friend, Montgomery, introduced Albert to John Brown because of a stolen horse that Albert had for sale.
>
> Therefore, there are a few elements that make this sign a necessity. First, Albert made sure that he died a martyr. He wrote to his friend, Rebecca Spring, and I paraphrase, that if he had ten thousand lives that he would give them all up in the name of freedom and liberty. Though he stayed on the run and argued in the court that they had the wrong man, he took responsibility in the end, and yet that didn't stop him from trying to play a corrupt system corruptly until he had to face his execution. Ultimately, Absalom Hazlett wanted to be remembered for something bigger than he was.

He paused and thought a bit. "Maybe that's what made Absalom Hazlett tick," Stephenson said.

"In closing, I will read the poem that he wrote the night before his death. In the morning, he slipped it to the only brother, Jonas, who visited him on that fateful day. He named it 'Hazlett's Farewell'":

Farewell my mother dear,
Do not mourn for me,
Remember that I die
In the cause of liberty

My time has come
To leave this earthly train;
Farewell my sister dear
We only part to meet again

Farewell my angelic maid,
So lovely, kind, and true,
I never will forget thee
In the land I'm going to

The crowd is hurrying to and fro,
The scaffold's reared on high,
Farewell kind friends one and all,
My time is drawing nigh

Farewell my dear old home,
I ne'er shall see it more,
My corpse will soon be hanging
On "Old Virgini's Shore"

Then my Spirit shall be gone
To the realms above,
Where we shall meet again
In the sphere of endless love.[4]

"Now, boys and girls," he said with a sigh, "I am tired of standing. I am going to sit down now." With that, Stephenson arduously made it back to his seat and sat down. The ceremony was wrapped up, so the kids got back on the bus and went back to school just in time for the dismissal bell to ring.

2

"Onward Christian Soldiers"

The Idea and Excavation (Summer of 1896–July 1899)

Absalom Hazlett was late to his own funeral, both of them. The first observance had to be postponed in Perth Amboy, New Jersey, while the bodies of the men of honor made it to town.

It was 1860, after the hanging of Hazlett and Aaron Stevens. The bodies were basically smuggled out of Charlestown, Virginia, and sent to Perth Amboy, New Jersey. There were alterations made to the proceedings and the transit of the bodies that were unannounced to avoid the agitated townspeople and protesters, who said they would destroy the coffins. In the streets of Perth Amboy stood out-of-state sectionalists who planned to demonstrate at the ceremonial, funeral-like burial of the remains, but the Raritan Bay Union communistic communal society, which Rebecca Spring organized, saw to it that a quaint and quiet affair went mostly unnoticed.

For the second funeral, almost forty years later, the attitudes were assuaged and the service to put all of Brown's men together in one memorial at his old farm in New York was given national attention. Miss Katherine Elizabeth McClellan jumped at the chance when she was asked to arrange the proceedings, and she vowed that the funeral would be unlike anything the residents had ever seen. Miss McClellan believed the service deserved national attention, so she envisioned a high-profile event as the "Chairman of the 'Committee of Arrangements' for the reinternment."[1]

Three men were responsible for starting the memorial at North Elba. Two of them were from Washington, D.C.: Dr. Thomas Featherstonhaugh and Captain E. P. Hall. The other man was a history professor at the University of Wisconsin, Dr. Orin G. Libby. Featherstonhaugh conceived the idea in 1896, and in July 1899, he, Hall, and Libby went to Harpers Ferry to excavate the mass grave.

When the eight raiders, who either died at the raid or were executed soon after, were exhumed at Harpers Ferry and a headstone was already erected for John Brown at his estate in New York, Dr. Featherstonhaugh began lining up participants to organize an affair to lay them all to rest together. He knew the perfect person for the job of making sure that the optics of the event would be just right. Thus, he drafted a letter to his artist friend, Miss McClellan:

> Yesterday, I raised all the remains, and they have started on their way to you in charge of Mr. Libby ... He seems rather peculiar and erratic, but enthusiastic over this matter. He will want the bones sneaked into the ground and nothing said about it, but I want some decent ceremonies to attend the burial that will make the matter memorable and historic.[2]

In her letter accepting the position to Dr. Featherstonhaugh, she wrote:

> This astounding proposition involving secrecy and risk ... appealed to my imagination ... I determined that no obstacle should deter me from giving these heroes the grand military funeral which would be a fitting climax for their sacrifice.[3]

She got to work right away, writing letters and making contacts to pull everything together and arrange an itinerary. Monday, August 28, 1899, was the date that was set. She wanted her guests of honor to be national dignitaries, like President McKinley, Vice President Hobart, and New York Governor Teddy Roosevelt. She was able to get Secretary of State Elihu Root to personally provide his consent to utilize a military detachment from the nearby federal barracks at Plattsburgh.[4]

With such an endorsement, the project began taking on a life of its own. With a smattering of newspaper coverage but mostly word-of-mouth and mentions of it in the neighboring churches, new efforts were made to get the two men buried in Eaglewood, New Jersey—Hazlett and Stevens—reassembled with their ideological kinsmen.

To make sure that there would be time to get all men together for the service, the date was pushed back a couple of days, so Miss McClellan's invitation sent to Professor Libby on August 25 read:

> Your presence is requested at the reinternment services of John Brown's followers, whose remains have recently been removed from Harpers Ferry to be placed beside their leader. The ceremonies will take place on Wednesday, August 30th, at 2 o'clock, p.m. at the John Brown Farm, North Elba, New York ... Conveyances will meet all trains.[5]

As luck would have it, and because timing is everything, the Perth Amboy tile company was looking for a way to get at the unique clay that lay underneath the topsoil of the cemetery where Hazlett and Stevens were buried. To be moved out of the way, some thought that the bodies were going to be sent to Kansas for burial, but when the project near Lake Placid was presented, the conflict seemed to resolve itself.

Brown biographer and admirer Richard J. Hinton and E. P. Stevens, nephew of the deceased, got permission to excavate the burial site. It took six men to do the work. H. Scott Wolfe documented the proceedings:

> The coffins were located at a depth of four feet and in order to preserve the skeletal remains, several men entered the grave to carefully scrape away the soil. Intact shoes came suddenly into view and a witness described what followed: "The principal bones of both bodies were found, although the femur of one of Stevens' leg was broken off ... Stevens' skull was about gone, but Hazlett's was minus only the face portion. The lower jaw bone of the latter was perfect and every tooth as sound as a dollar." The clothing was in a decent stare of preservation, "the left lapel of (Hazlett's) black cloth coat was brought up, wet and soggy, but otherwise in good condition." The workers observed numerous buttons and the gum rubber coat in which the remains of Stevens had been wrapped. Small pieces of this coat, still remarkably elastic, were cut off as souvenirs by those present ...
>
> A large pine box, packed with sawdust and partitioned to separate the two men, was filled with the surviving bones, bits of cloth and leather and the earth taken from the respective body cavities. The box was sealed and immediately prepared for shipment, its label bearing the address.
>
> The John Brown Homestead, North Elba, Essex Co., N.Y.
> Care Katherine E. McClellan
> Chairman, Committee (Reinterment) of Arrangements[6]

It just so happened that the date marked the forty-third anniversary of the Battle of Osawatomie, and because the box with the remains of the two from New Jersey did not arrive by the time they were ready to start the preliminary procession, the ceremonies had to begin without them.

Flashback to How Eight Raiders Were Thrown in a Box (October 16, 17, and 18, 1859)

Of the twenty-two men that took part in the raid, seven were immediately captured and hanged, five escaped and dispersed, and ten were eventually caught up with and brought to justice by penalties of death. Of the ten killed at Harpers Ferry, eight were gathered together, thrown in a single casket, and buried in a 3-foot hole at the foot of the Shenandoah River. Those left on the bank of the Shenandoah were Oliver Brown, William and Dauphin Thompson, Stewart Taylor, John Henry Kagi, William H. Leeman, and the two black men that joined the group: Dangerfield Newby and Lewis Sheridan Leary.

Watson Brown and Jeremiah Anderson, because they were such physical specimens, were given to the visiting physicians from the medical school in Winchester, Virginia.

Two of Brown's sons died during the raid—Watson and Oliver. His other son, Owen, was stationed at the farmhouse and eluded authorities. Owen ended up being the last of the Harpers Ferry raiders to die on January 9, 1899, in Pasadena, California.

Watson was tall and described as "good looking" with chiseled features like his dad but lacking in the dark characteristics and features that hinted at insanity. He was born on October 7, 1835. In the attack that took place that Monday morning at the Engine House in Harpers Ferry, Watson found himself out-matched and exposed in the street with Aaron Stevens. They began waving white flags of surrender, but because the band's intentions were well-known and the townspeople were hell-bent on making an example of the coup, they fired on the two. Both of the men were wounded. Stevens and Watson were able to seek shelter in the Engine House where his father was wounded and dying.

That afternoon, the engine house was stormed by the citizens and Watson was said to have "fought as brave as ever any man fought," according to a letter written by Edwin Coppoc. The small group of men hunkered down and neutralized the attack, but Watson apparently fought so hard that he expended himself. Almost immediately after the clash, he fell ill and was unable to walk. On Tuesday, Robert E. Lee and J. E. B. Stuart's cavalry arrived to restore order with their first target being the Engine House, where Brown was reported to be. "When we were taken in the morning," Coppoc wrote, "he was just able to walk."[7] Due to his condition, his father sent him out with a white flag of surrender. He dispatched Aaron Stevens to go with him. Both were fired upon again, this time by Martinsburg troops from Virginia, and both made it back inside the Engine House. Stevens was shot four times, but lived to be captured, jailed, and executed. Watson, on the other hand, was shot in his lower abdomen. He writhed in agonizing pain and begged for someone to put him out of his misery. When no one helped, he put a pistol to his head to commit suicide. His father stopped him and calmed him. Coppoc wrote that he continued getting worse from then until about 3 o'clock Wednesday morning when he died.

Oliver was Brown's youngest son, born four years after Watson, on March 9, 1839. He was shot and killed by citizens that Monday morning when Watson fell. There was time to drag him into the Engine House, but he was near death and expired soon after.

There was another set of brothers, William and Dauphin Thompson. Their father, Roswell Thompson, owned the land next to Brown. Their sister, Isabella, married Watson. They had another brother named Henry, and he was married to Brown's oldest daughter, Ruth. She was able to convince Henry not to follow his brothers to Harpers Ferry.

As a messenger, William was sent early Monday morning to tell the three stationed at headquarters, the Kennedy farmhouse in Maryland, that the plan had gone haywire and that they were to remove the weapons and supplies and go on to the schoolhouse—the Plan "B" exit strategy. As William returned Tuesday morning to the Engine House to report back to Brown, he was captured by Lee's soldiers, who were sent by President James Buchanan. William found that his brother had been shot and killed while trying to protect Brown and the ideal. The troops took him to be held for justice at the inn in town, but an angry mob seized him from the hotel and began a procession to the bridge across the Potomac. Once there, they stood him on the edge and executed him. His body fell into the water.

There was one other man who weathered the Monday morning fracas but was shot and wounded that afternoon—Stewart Taylor, who was the only raider not born in America. He was from Uxbridge, Canada, and he was so spiritual that he had premonitions. He saw it his destiny that he would die in Harpers Ferry, fighting for the abolitionist cause. Leading up to the raid, Taylor lost touch with Brown and had not heard any details about the plans and his involvement, so Taylor panicked and tried to get back into contact with the old man. He was relieved when he got word to meet Brown that August at the farmhouse. In the course of planning and organizing, the men had a disagreement and disbanded. Stewart was disappointed and feared that the idea had completely dissolved and that he would miss his date with destiny. So, when the team put aside their differences and reunited, Stewart was the first to be right at Brown's side to play his part in the raid.

That Monday afternoon during the counterattack of the townspeople, Stewart was shot and wounded. After hours of agonizing pain, suffering, and begging his compadres to put him out of his misery, he died at the doors of the engine house. His lifeless body served as a barrier the next morning when "the Virginians" tried to break down the door. Stewart Taylor was twenty-three when he died, just as he predicted.

The youngest raider to take part in the raid, however, was William Henry Leeman. He left home without telling his mother anything about the raid, but soon before the event, he wrote her to tell her of his intentions and why this cause was so important. Leeman was watching from the armory yard when Watson and Stevens were fired upon when trying to surrender. The frightening realization that the townspeople wanted blood and were taking no prisoners drove him to jump the fence and run for the Potomac. He jumped in the water and tried to swim to the other side in an attempt to escape; however, not a strong swimmer and weighted down with boots and clothing, he began drowning and waving for help in the water.

One of the townsmen on the other side waded out in the water and got Leeman onto a small islet; as Leeman tried to recover on his hands and knees, the man pulled out a revolver and shot him in the head. He collapsed on the rocks, and that was where his body would lay. His body remained on the islet that night and was used as target practice by townspeople and the militia all the next day. When his mother heard of his death and how his remains were treated, she went into shock and lay in bed for eighteen months, unable to speak.[8]

Desecrating the bodies of the men was a symbolic gesture by the townsfolk manifested by the fear and paranoia that spreads from terrorism and the disgust and ire for the audacity to buck an institution. Yet, it was that same fear and disgust for the institution that prompted Jeremiah Goldsmith Anderson, a grandson of slaveholders, to join Brown in the raid. What happened to his remains after his death is a stark reminder of the evil humans can do to each other.

Ironically enough, Jeremiah Anderson's calling was to combat evil by becoming a preacher. He was born in Putnam County, Wisconsin, on April 13, 1833. He was intelligent and studied hard, but he ended up buying farmland in Kansas in his mid-twenties, instead of going on to higher learning. In Kansas, Anderson met John Brown and became one of his most ardent disciples. He trusted and believed in Brown and believed that they would "win at all costs," as he said in a letter to his brother.[9] He was with Brown throughout the entire process—at the farmhouse, at the raid, and at the Engine House when it was stormed by the militia. When troops charged the Engine House that Tuesday morning, Anderson threw himself at the doors; he was bayonetted and "dragged out of the building vomiting gore."[10]

As he lay dying, an armed farmer approached him, forced his mouth open with his boot, and spat a huge quid of tobacco into his mouth.[11] He was savagely kicked in the body and in the face and left a bloody mess in the street.

Perhaps the worst atrocity was committed against Dangerfield Newby. At forty-four, Newby was the oldest raider and the first raider to die at Harpers Ferry. Depending on who was telling the story, Newby can be called a "mulatto," a "mixed-breed," or a "half-breed." Dangerfield's father was Henry Newby, a wealthy Scottish landowner in Fauquier County. His mother was Elsey Newby, a slave owned by Henry's neighbor, John Fox. Henry and Elsey lived together for years under the guise of a slave-and-master relationship because interracial relationships were against Virginia law. Dangerfield was their first child, and they ended up having several children together.

Dangerfield later married Harriet Newby, who was owned by Jesse Jennings of the neighboring county of Warrenton. The two fell in love and began raising a family. Goaded by the pangs of remorse and guilt of slavery, Henry Newby moved the family to Bridgeport, Ohio, and claimed their emancipation. When Dangerfield returned to Warrenton to buy his wife's freedom, Jennings said that $1,500 was the cost. After time passed and the money was raised, Dangerfield returned to buy Harriet and their baby's freedom, willing to sacrifice the other children, who was at working age and intended to be bought later, but Jennings upped the price and refused to sell Harriet and the baby. Broken-hearted, Dangerfield vowed that he would find a way to free his entire family, and that is when he heard of John Brown.

There were a lot of rifles produced and housed in Harpers Ferry, but it was said that there was little ammunition available. So, in the first morning of the raid, one man was loading 6-inch spikes into the rifle, and it was one of these spikes that caught Newby and cut his throat from "ear to ear."[12] Newby was killed instantly.

There is a street in town called "Hog Alley," and this is how it got its name. Newby's body was stomped, stabbed, and mutilated by the townspeople. They wanted to make an example of him, so they cut off his arms, and one man sliced off his ears as souvenirs. They beat his body with sticks and turned the hogs on his body. Joseph Barry was an eyewitness of the account; he later wrote:

> Shortly after Newby's death a hog came up, rooted around the spot where the body lay and at first appeared to be unconscious that anything extraordinary was in its way. After a while, the hog paused and snuffed around it and put its snout to the dead man's face. Suddenly, the brute was apparently seized with a panic, and with bristles erect and drooping tail, it scampered away, as if for dear life. This display did not, however, deter others of the same species from crowding around the corpse and literally devouring it. The writer saw all this with his own eyes, as the saying is, and at the risk of further criticism, he will remark that none of the good people of Harpers Ferry appeared to be at all squeamish about the quality of flavor of their pork that winter.[13]

Some historians marginalize the contributions that black people gave to such rebellions, playing on the stereotype of the docile slave content with their master. The fact of the matter, however, is that Brown was able to garner the support of former and brave slaves in confinement. In retelling the tale to build a case that black people could not be counted on to help, it is left out by many accounts that John Kagi chose Leary and Copeland as brave companions to secure the Rifle Works with him.

Lewis Sheridan Leary, like Newby, was a free black man. He was born in Fayetteville, North Carolina, to free parents. Repelled by conditions in the south, he moved to Oberlin, Ohio, where he met Brown when following an abolitionist movement in Cleveland. Leary convinced his nephew, John Anthony Copeland, to join Brown's cause. The two were part of phase two of the plan—to secure Hall's Rifle Works and wait for it to be cleared out of stock.

John Henry Kagi was twenty-four, but he was given credit by many as the most educated and intelligent of the entire clan. He was a newspaper correspondent for eastern newspapers, a stenographer for the courts, an educator and teacher in Hawkinstown, Virginia (now West Virginia), and a lawyer, but the men called him the "Secretary of War."

If Brown wanted a solid opinion or was in need of counsel, it was Kagi that he turned to for advice. Kagi believed that the men would be able to sneak into town, ambush the United States Armory and Arsenal at Harpers Ferry, and steal away into the early morning hours into the mountains before the townspeople awoke without even knowing that they were there. He did not know that word of the raid had spread and that the townspeople were just waiting to see if the rumors were true.

Kagi was born in Ohio, but he taught in Hawkinstown, Virginia; there, he was introduced to the institution of slavery. From there, he moved to study law and was admitted to the bar in Nebraska. While in Nebraska, he helped his sister and brother-in-law to build a cave to be part of the Underground Railroad. Moved by the events taking place in Kansas, he joined up with Aaron Stevens' Second Kansas Militia. Through Stevens, Kagi met John Brown, and the two became fast friends and confidants. Brown said that he admired that he was an agnostic, "course in fiber, cold in manner, and rough in appearance."[14] Never half-cocked, he gave thoughtful, straight, no-holds-barred advice, and Brown trusted that and respected his insightful candor.

Kagi and Stevens were at the head of the two lines that the men walked in formation from the farm in Maryland into town that Sunday night of the raid, and they were the first to cross the bridge to Harpers Ferry. Tidd and Cook cut the telegraph lines, and the Engine House was taken. Once that phase was complete, Kagi, Copeland, and others went to Hall's Rifle Factory.

Kagi had the important task of the Rifle Works, which was about half a mile down the road from the Engine House along the Shenandoah. Clever, quick, and determined, Kagi secured the Rifle Works and awaited further orders, but by that morning, news spread like wildfire that the town was under siege, and the townspeople sparked a rebellion of their own. In the morning, war broke out, but the men were able to hold their ground. Lee's men came to town, stormed the Engine House, and turned their attention on the Rifle Works by that afternoon. This new resurgence was more than what Kagi and his men could handle.

Kagi escaped out the back, jumping into the Shenandoah River to retreat into the mountains. He was near the middle when he was struck by a hail of bullets and left floating face down in the water. In his escape, Leary was badly wounded, captured, and held in the carpenter's shop, where he died a few hours after suffering excruciating pain. By many accounts, Lee's Virginians were said to have shown the dying man pity and compassion before his passing, even relating his dying wish to his family. He wanted them to know that "I am ready to die."[15]

Copeland in his escape from the Rifle Works was soon captured, tried, and found guilty of murder and conspiring with slaves to rebel. He was hanged on December 16, 1859.

When peace and order were restored in the town, the bodies were picked from the streets and rivers. Burial was refused by all the churches and cemeteries in the town, so a resident, James Mansfield, was given $5 to bury the eight bodies. Dr. Featherstonhaugh wrote:

> He procured two large "store boxes" and into these receptacles thrust the remains of the eight men, and buried them about half a mile from the ferry upon the bands of the Shenandoah River, almost a the water's edge. Here they remained, unmarked and almost unknown, until July 29, 1899, when the writer, accompanied by Captain E.P. Hall of Washington and Professor O.G. Libby of the University of Wisconsin, exhumed the remains, which were at once carried to North Elba by Dr. Libby. The two great boxes were found some three feet below the surface of the ground. They were, of course, much decayed, but from being constantly wet, by proximity to the river, were remarkably preserved. Most of the smaller bones had crumbled away, but the long bones of the men were recovered.[16]

The Funeral (August 30, 1899)

The funeral procession—with military escort and preceded by the Saranac Lake Cornet Band—departed the Opera House Block, Lake

Placid, at 1.30 p.m.[17] The invited dignitaries did not attend, but there were supporters gathered to pay their respects and finally put to rest the martyrs that represented something greater as a collective group, rather than as individuals. Newspapers from around the country covered the sensationalized incident at Harpers Ferry, but only a handful seemed to cover this event, though those who were in attendance gave varying estimates as to the number of supporters there. Some papers reported that 1,000 walked or were in carriages in procession. Some reported that by the end when all were assembled there were 2,000 in full attendance, and others reported over 3,000 showed solidarity in the cause of liberation.

Whatever the attendance numbers, they all worked in unison to honor the men and what they stood for, and all in attendance joined in the singing of "Onward Christian Soldiers," "My Country 'Tis of Thee," and "John Brown's Body."

It was stifling hot, but the men and women dressed in their Sunday best to show their respects. Episcopal Bishop Henry Potter oversaw the program and introduced each speaker. Bishop Potter was a short, balding man with stern, tired eyes. The few strands of hair on the top of his head were too few to use as a comb-over, but there was enough to create a distraction and give the impression of a hairline.

In 1893, Bishop Potter gave an address for a dedication of a monument at Gettysburg for the fallen Union soldiers of his home state of New York, and he ruffled feathers with his controversial view that God's divine justice intervened to grant victory for the Union. Ms. McClellan asked him to speak at this affair and introduce the speakers:

> Ladies and gentlemen, thank you for being here today to celebrate a notion. That notion that regardless of the laws of mortal men, our duty is to follow God's plan. Is it a sin to break a sinful law? No. Laws of God supersede laws of man. Here laid before us ten individuals to be held in honor because they were smart enough, brave enough, and motivated enough to follow John Brown's crusade of spreading freedom across this land, a God-granted right of every man, woman, and child. And, John Brown sought to defend it. These ten men fought to defend it, and the proof that they have won is that God granted us this joyous occasion today.
>
> You see, even though they died not seeing the end of slavery, they helped bring an end to it by bringing about the Civil War. Because of the War, slaves were freed, and God's justice was levied. We must remember that God willed Union victory as we age away from the horrendousness of the Civil War, which John Brown and these men brought forth. We may never forget which the cause was substantially decided here was the cause of freedom, and justice, and the everlasting equities, as against of

> despotism which, however amiable it ordinary exhibitions had in it ... the essence of that "crime that degrades men." We may never forget that behind the question of unpaid labor, of bartered manhood, of a traffic which dealt in human hearts.[18]
>
> To honor and eulogize the men, we have Mr. Whitelaw Reid. Mr. Reid has been Editor in Chief of *The New York Tribune*, and it can be argued that *The New York Tribune* is the most influential newspaper in the United States since 1872. Seven years ago, Mr. Reid ran as Vice President for Benjamin Harrison, and before running on that ticket he served as Minister to France for seven years leading up to the election. Mr. Reid has proven himself a man of peace. Last year, he worked under President William McKinley on the commission that negotiated peace after the Spanish-American War. So, please welcome Mr. Reid.

Reid took the podium and thanked Bishop Potter for his introduction. He had a thick, heavy mustache that came down over both lips. After a few minutes of polite words, Reid began his conclusion:

> I do see the need for peace in a civil society, but I also understand why John Brown and his men disrupted peace in our own country to call attention to a serious problem in our republic. For that, I am thankful.
>
> I am also very thankful for the bravery that it took to buck the system and put their lives on the line for a cause. In my business, editors and journalists need to muster this type of bravery. There is not one who dares to express an honest opinion. If you express it, you would know beforehand that it would never appear in print. I am paid $150 (a week) for keeping honest opinions out of the paper with which I am connected ... The business of the New York journalist is to distort the truth, lie outright, to pervert, to vilify, to fawn ot [*sic.*] the feet of mammon, and to sell his country and his race for this daily bread, or for what is about the same thing, his salary. You know this and I know it ... We are tools and vassals of the rich men behind the scenes. We are jumping jacks. They pull the strings and we dance. Our time, our talents, our lives, our possibilities are all the property of other men. We are intellectual prostitutes.[19] In contrast, these men that we are here to reinter stood true to their ideals and gave the ultimate price for their principles.

There was stunned applause. Then, Bishop Potter reclaimed the stage to pass it on to Reverend Joshua Young:

> We could not conclude today without hearing from another man who made a tremendous sacrifice for his beliefs when he presided over the

funeral of John Brown on December 8, 1859. Next month will mark the fortieth anniversary of Reverend Young's dedication at John Brown's ceremony, and we are happy that he could make it here today.

Reverend Young spoke next:

Thank you, Bishop Potter, let us bow our heads. Almighty and most merciful God, we lift our souls unto thee and bow our hearts to the unutterable emotions of his impressive hour ... Our souls are filled with awe and are subdued to silence, as we think of the great reverential, heroic soul, whose mortal remains are now to commit to the earth, "dust to dust," while his spirit dwells with God who gave it, and his memory is enshrined in every pure and holy heart ... O! hasten on the day when no more wrong or injustice shall be done in the earth; when all men shall love one another with pure hearts, fervently, and love with all their strength; which we ask in the name and as the disciples of Jesus Christ. Amen.[20]

Almost 40 years ago, I gave that exact same prayer. The day that was a pivotal moment in my life. I told the story from Matthew 12:12 that day. Remember that is the story of Jesus breaking the law of Sabbath in order to help and heal a human from suffering. But it was Timothy 4:7-8 that created a firestorm. "I have fought a good fight, I have finished my course, I have kept the faith. Henceforth there is laid up for me a crown of righteousness which the righteous judge shall give me the day, and not to me only, but unto all them also that love is appearing."

The next day, my hometown newspaper in Burlington transcribed my speech and attacked me for using that passage in the context of John Brown. Though no one took my life, my livelihood in Burlington, Vermont was taken. "I suffered the fate of all pronounced abolition preachers, returning from the grave of John Brown a social outcast, not fit to live, certainly not fit to occupy the pulpit, but must be driven out as I was. Cast out into the world with a certain stigma upon me for my sympathy with a felon for who family in distress I had dared to pray and had no apology."[21]

As a result, the congregation voted no-confidence in my ministry, and I resigned from my post because I had confidence in knowing that I had done the right thing as a Unitarian. As one door closes, one door opens, and I went on to work to spread God's word in other churches, finally landing in Groton, Massachusetts, where I am today.

I have found a home and been with the people in Groton the past twenty-four years. When it was learned that these remains were being transported and interred here at North Elba, it was my church that urged me to take "charge of the religious ceremonies" here today.[22]

> I would like to credit time for changing and softening the attitudes towards these heroes, but the fact of the matter is that there will always be those that see Brown and these men as madmen, as terrorists, as villains as opposed to the men of God that they were.

Reverend Young wrapped up the ceremony, and thirty-two members of the 26th U.S. Infantry fired three shots over the soldiers before "Taps" was played. All the speakers and honorary guests gathered together for pictures before they departed to dine. That evening, the remains of Hazlett and Stevens arrived in a trunk, and they were finally laid to rest with their brethren.

3

The 10,000 Lives of Absalom Hazlett

News Report of the Sentence (February 20, 1860)

The *Fayetteville Semi-Weekly Observer,* as did many other newspapers across the country, ran a quick blip from the wire. It read, "*Harpers Ferry Executions*—The convicted insurgents, Stevens and Hazlett will be hanged on Friday, March 16. They deny guilt and charge prosecuting witnesses with perjury."

A Plug of Tobacco (End of February to Mid-March 1860)

If historians want to point to the incident at Harpers Ferry as the catalyst to the Civil War, then the case of Absalom Hazlett was the specific case that concretely served as a litmus test for the division of the nation. Petitions from Pennsylvania, Ohio, Massachusetts, and as far as Canada were signed by thousands asking for the pardon of Hazlett. The appeal from his hometown of Indiana, Pennsylvania, was said to be a very long list of signatures asking for the clemency of "Absalom or Albert Hazlett, the son of an aged and widowed mother, whose last years will be lengthened and cheered." Another from Carlisle was very similar in that it said, "his poor, heart-broken old mother, whose life seems bound up in that of this her next youngest but erring son."[1]

Judge Graham of Cumberland County wrote a letter to the Governor of Virginia. He asked for clemency and said that he not only wrote on behalf of "many of our most worthy and estimable citizens, but from the promptings of my own feelings."[2] In his letter, he said that he had cooperated fully with the wishes of Virginia and so asked for the same consideration. He went on to say that in his observance of Hazlett while in the Carlisle jail, his interactions with the many visitors who spent time with him while he awaited judgment, and his overall demeanor, Hazlett was "not the bold, bad-hearted young man but had been made the dupe of Brown ... I am confident that all 5,000 men of our community would be very much gratified if you would extend the hand of executive clemency to this erring and unfortunate young man Hazlett who was excited so much sympathy in our county."[3]

Another letter came from Carlisle, one from Frederick Watts, the representative of the Virginian claimants in the extradition trial. He said, "Hazlett's pardon would be responded to in this community as an act of magnanimity on the part of Virginia...It would afford me great satisfaction to learn that your Excellency had taken this view of the Subject."[4]

Some fifty-five Pennsylvania state legislators from the House and Senate signed a petition dated March 13. A Representative Taylor made mention that they were out of session, otherwise many more names would've been on the signature list. The petition read:

> Whereas considerable interest is felt in the fate of young Pennsylvanian, Albert Hazlett, lately convicted in Charlestown, Virginia, and sentenced to be hanged on the 16th inst. for participating in the deplorable John Brown raid upon the State of Virginia; Your petitioners, in consideration of this sympathy, founded upon the representation that Hazlett is a young, simple-minded man, likely to have been influenced by John Brown, in ignorance of the enormity of the crime he may have committed, would respectfully ask ... that ... Your Excellency will be pleased if not to pardon, at least to commute his sentence to a milder punishment than that of death.[5]

Those abolitionists who had little hope that legal appeals to the state of Virginia would free Hazlett made plans to break him out of jail. There are several documented attempts and other rumored attempts made to free Hazlett. Even before being sentenced in Charlestown, there was a conspiracy to break Hazlett out of jail in Carlisle while he awaited extradition.

His old mentor from the "Bleeding Kansas" days, James Montgomery, was orchestrating an elaborate plan to break Hazlett out. He elicited the help of Richard J. Hinton, John W. LeBarnes, and Thomas Wentworth Higginson. Higginson went to work rounding up the necessary weapons—revolvers he got on loan. The others began raising funding that was needed to pull off such a deposition. Wendell Phillips, an anti-slavery activist from Boston, promised $200; artist and sculptor E. A. Brackett $200; and Colonel D. R. Anthony of Leavenworth, Kansas, $300.[6] Higginson also approached Rebecca Smith for funding, and she was able to get Mrs. Brown to tap into the benefit funds raised from the sale of James Redpath's book *The Life of John Brown*. Overall, it was estimated that over $2,000 was raised to cover the expense of gathering information and positioning themselves to break Hazlett and Stevens out of confinement.

The group met in Harrisburg at the home of Dr. William Rutherford. Montgomery was dispatched to the "vicinity of Charlestown and Silas C. Soule, who had a perfect southern accent, went into Charlestown itself in the guise of an Irishman."[7] Soon, playing on the stereotype, the townspeople got to recognize him as a town drunk.

Soule had reddish-brown hair and a sparse beard that highlighted his paleness and grew on the bottom of his chin but not on his cheeks. His facial hair accentuated his youthful characteristics with a faint mustache that refused to grow in fully. One night, Soule went into a local pub and began acting out as if he had too much to drink. He continued to cause such a commotion that the sheriff had to be called to take him away and put him in jail to sleep it off. There, he got the opportunity to talk to Stevens and Hazlett.

"We're working on a plan to get you guys out of here," Soule whispered.

"Not going to happen," Hazlett said in hushes. "There are at least eighty men standing guard at any one time. Escape is impossible."

"We are armed and ready," asserted Soule.

Stevens walked up close to Soule and pleaded, "Abandon this mission. No more innocent people should be killed in our name. It is over for us. Please, sir, report back to the others that this mission is over." Then Soule, Stevens, and Hazlett inched to the back corner of the cell. Soule slumped over as if in a drunken stupor, and the other two continued making a case for discontinuing any attempts to break them out of jail.

"Please do me a favor when you return," Hazlett said to Soule. "I have a personal message for Mr. Hinton. Please tell him that I said farewell and thank you for all that he has done for me and our great cause. I have never forgotten or overlooked the fact that he was a great friend to me." Soule nodded and pretended to pass out and go to sleep.

The next morning, Soule was taken before the magistrate and given a reprimand for his drunken and disorderly behavior and warned to not return to the jail or face a longer sentence. He and Montgomery returned to Harrisburg and relayed all messages.

The group of abolitionists took Soule's report and the wishes of Stevens and Hazlett to heart. Later, Higginson wrote that the effort was deserted "partly because" the two did not want to "endanger the life of the jailer, Avis, who had won their gratitude, as well as Brown's, by his great kindness."[8]

Some in the group wanted to persist and return to free Stevens and Hazlett, but as it turned out, heavy snows and extreme cold blanketed any and all attempts to free the two prisoners. It was decided by vote of the party to abandon the expedition altogether.[9]

William Shearer also detailed an attempt to free Hazlett, which Hazlett unwittingly or knowingly foiled himself. On the night before the November 5 hearing, Shearer and another defense attorney were visiting with Hazlett to iron out the details for the next day's proceedings. They sat in the conference room that was in the front of the building off from the main lobby. The cells were in the back. It was about 10 o'clock in the evening when they began wrapping up.

"I think that it is only fair for you to know that I was with John Brown in Kansas, and I fought right along beside him in several battles," Hazlett confessed.

"That is all fine and dandy," said Shearer, "but that is none of our business. That has no bearing on what we are trying to do here, this particular case." Shearer and the other attorney began cleaning up and stacking their papers, packing up to call it a night. While doing so, they were distracted by Hazlett.

"Mr. Shearer," he said, "on your way out, could you tell the sheriff that I would like to have a plug of tobacco?"

"Certainly, Mr. Harrison," Shearer agreed, calling Hazlett by the only name that the county, the courts, and those making the arrest knew him as: William Harrison. On the way out of the conference room, Shearer stopped by Sheriff McCartney's desk and relayed the message. "Mr. Harrison requests from you a plug of tobacco," he said.

He later wrote about the incident: "Now it is remarkable on what small matters one's life may depend. Asking for that plug of tobacco cost that man his life," for when McCartney went back to the cell, he found that someone had busted out the back of it. A blanket served as a thin veil against the damage. Hazlett was resituated in a more secure location to quell any further attempts of mischievousness. It was later determined that Mark Scott, an African American barber, was sent to Carlisle by a follower of John Brown with a horse and buggy, a rope ladder, and instructions to help Hazlett make his escape.[10]

The next morning, McCartney went up to Shearer and said, "That client of yours is the most stupid man I ever saw in my life. You know when I was sent down with him, it was very dark, as dark as midnight, and if he would've just given me a little push I would have fallen over in the gutter. He could have been out in the North Mountains in a short time."[11] The statement solidified Shearer's suspicions. McCartney was sympathetic to the man and his cause and was willing to allow him to slip through his fingers. The request for tobacco could be interpreted as a warning to the sheriff to make him wise to the fact that the people that he was associated with had the ways and means to free him. It could also be interpreted that Hazlett was, indeed, giving up without further bloodshed.

There was one other scheme that involved Albert's brother, Jonas, who was regularly mistaken for his twin. Jonas shaved his beard to look even more like Albert and was said to have wanted to take his brother's place. In Albert's letters to him, he had said that he regretted the fact that he could not marry his one and only true love, Miss Stevens, Aaron's sister, and have children. Jonas intended to give him that opportunity, so he slipped into the cell and urged his brother to leave as the visitor. Albert refused, saying, "No, I have helped strike the blow to free slaves, and I will die for that right."[12]

A Little Sympathy Goes a Long Way in Prison (March 1, 1860)

From jail, Hazlett wrote a letter to Anne Brown:

> My Dear Friend Anne,
>
> Your kind letter game [*sic.*] me much pleasure to know there was some who had sympathy for me in my prison home. I am thankful to you for your kind and cheering letter to me. Do not grieve about the past, but take all things for the best. I think, as you do, that my fate is hard and very unjust. But I shall try to meet it like a man. I do not see that my death will do them any good, but "the Lord's will, not mine be done." I do not think the citizens here thirst for my blood; they have treated me very kind and humane; the ladies come in to see us most every day, and gentlemen also, Good-bye, Anne, I am your friend.
>
> W. H. Harrison[13]

Hazlett's Plea: "Bury Me in a Free Land" (March 15, 1860)

There's an old narrative poem by Robert Service called "The Cremation of Sam McGee." In that poem, a gold miner in the Klondike from Tennessee named Sam McGee knows that he is about to die in the cold of the North Pole, so before he dies, he asks his buddy to do him a favor. It reads:

> It's the cursed cold, and it got right hold till I'm chilled clean through to the bone. Yet tain't being dead—it's my awful dread of the icy grave that pains; So, I want you to swear that, foul or fair, you'll cremate my last remains.

Just like that, the narrator is burdened with the curse of carrying out Sam McGee's dying wish. This forges an existential bond that then binds the two together. The narrator said, "A pal's last need is a thing to heed, so I swore I would not fail," and with bad weather closing in, rations getting low, and his sled dogs exhausted by the extra load of the dead Sam McGee, the narrator trudges on until he comes across the materials to start a fire because, after all, "a promise made is a debt unpaid." The ending of the poem takes a weird, supernatural twist. In comparison, Hazlett's story also has its quirky narrative turns.

Like Sam McGee, Absalom had one dying wish too—not to be buried in slave country. With his family too poor to fulfill his last request, he turned to a fellow abolitionist that gave him comfort as a pen pal, Miss Rebecca Spring. She was a sympathizer that befriended all the jailed raiders as they stood trial, and as one by one the men were hanged, she did all that she could to raise awareness of their cause and to solidify their martyrdom. In a letter, Hazlett requested that she take his "last remains" out of the south.

She was an integral lifeline in corresponding and helping to build a case for John Brown and his men. Stevens and Hazlett were the last in line. In documenting the incident in her personal memoir, she wrote:

> When all hope of mercy was over, he wrote to ask me to have him buried with Mr. Stevens, in a free land. He sent me the following lines written by a colored woman:[14]

"Bury Me in a Free Land"

Make me a grave wher'er you will,
In a lowly plain, on a lofty hill;
It among earth's humblest graves,
But not in a land where men are slaves.

I ask no monument proud and high,
To arrest the gaze of the passers by;
All that my yearning spirit craves,
Is-Bury me not in a Land of Slaves.

With time slipping away, Mrs. Spring wrote back to Absalom and, indeed, promised that she would see to it that he and Stevens would be taken out of Virginia and laid to rest in the free north, so on the night before his execution, he was solemn but prepared to die. With dignity and stoicism, he wrote to Miss Spring, praying that the note would reach her hands, since he had no way to assure it. The date was March 15, 1860, and he wrote:

Dear Friend:

Your letter gave me comfort to know that my body would be taken from this land of chains. You spoke of my friends; I never wrote to them, but my brother has come to see me. He left the matter to me, and I thought it best to let you have my body. You wanted to know who were [*sic.*] dear to me; I say everybody that is good is dear to me. I am willing to die in the cause of liberty; if I had ten thousand lives, I would willingly lay them all down for the same cause. My death will do more good than if I had lived.

Farewell, my dear friend,
W. H. Harrison[15]

At the Gallows (March 16, 1860)

In the morning of the execution, Stevens and Hazlett asked their jailor, Avis, if they could have breakfast together. They had built a relationship with the man over their long days in their cells, and Avis had grown sympathetic to their cause, getting to know the men as men. Stevens had friends visiting, including his sister and wife, and Hazlett's brother Jonas came too in support, bringing a cheerful nature to the dismal day.

Avis arranged the tables in the wide hallway so that all could be seated together. He took the irons and shackles from the men's hands and feet and allowed them to sit down one last time in dignity. During the meal, with the men preparing the scaffold in clear sight through the window, the women broke down from time to time in heavy sobs. Stevens encouraged them to be strong saying, "Keep up your heart just a little longer."[16]

They finished their meal, and it was time to say their final goodbyes. Stevens hugged and kissed his sister and then grabbed his wife in a tight embrace. She wept. Not for one moment did he show any weakness, but he said to Avis, "Get them away as soon as you can, I can't bear this much longer."[17]

There was a carriage waiting outside the jailhouse, and Avis ushered the visitors out and into the carriage. Hazlett's brother paused. He realized that he had forgotten something and had to go back inside the prison. What he saw shook him to his core. He saw the "mortal agony only God was expected to see," as Rebecca Spring put it.[18]

Soon after the carriage disappeared over the horizon, the men were taken to the scaffold. As in the case with the hanging of John Brown about three and a half months before, the execution of Stevens and Hazlett was staged as a final, impressive Virginia military display and a gala spectacle for the public.[19] Twelve military companies were dispatched to the event with five lining the walkway from the jail to the scaffold, and there were seven that surrounded the platform.

There were reporters there to document the event, but only minor details separate their accounts of the procession to the scaffold and the actual execution. All accounts noted that both prisoners seemed at ease and even at times nodded to acknowledge some people in the crowd as they passed by; they also spoke to guards and authorities that were near.

It was 12.15 p.m. when they made it up the steps with Sheriff Campbell, Avis, the jail guard J. W. Gallaher, and others who worked at the jail. One of the most detailed reports came from *The Virginia Free Press*:

> Stevens stepped his foot upon the trap and made some remark which we did not hear, but he spoke smilingly. Hazlett seemed a good deal agitated and as soon as he got upon the scaffold commenced bidding the Sheriff and others "goodbye." A moment or two elapsed whilst the necessary arrangements for the execution were completed, which was improved by the culprits in making a survey of the crowd in attendance. Stevens and Hazlett noticing the little sons of Jailor Avis immediately below them, called them by name and bid them "good-bye," and bowed to others whom they recognized in the crowd. The ropes and the cowls now adjusted, and they were led forward upon the trap that was to launch them into eternity. Immediately before the cowl was drawn down over his face, Hazlett caught Stevens by the hand, bid him "good bye," embraced and kissed him, Stevens then turned to Jailor Avis, caught him by the hand and said, "Farewell, I shall never forget your kindness."
>
> The ropes being adjusted to the hook, Stevens said, "be quick. Let us know when you are ready." Just then the drop fell, and Stevens and Hazlett were ushered into the unknown hereafter. Hazlett died comparatively without a struggle, but Stevens writhed in violent contortions for several minutes, the knot of the noose having slipped behind the ear.
>
> After hanging 30 minutes, Drs. Mason and Starry examined the bodies and pronounced life extinct. They were immediately cut down and placed in neat walnut coffins, enclosed in cases, and directed to Marcus Spring, South Amboy, New Jersey, per Adams Express, and were sent to Harpers Ferry by Mr. George Sandler, the undertaker, and given into the charge of the friends who had taken leave of them that morning.[20]

It was later detailed in Richard Hinton's authoritative work *John Brown and His Men* what it was that Stevens said to his jailor. As he mounted the gallows and stepped on the trap, he got Avis's attention and said so only he could hear, "Captain, remember I had won the first choice!"[21]

Rebecca Spring Keeps Her Promise (March 19, 1860)

As Albert requested, Mrs. Spring had the two walnut boxes that held the bodies shipped to New Jersey. Their point of entry had to be altered because of rumors that an angry mob waited to toss their coffins overboard.[22]

Those in attendance were the staunchest of abolitionists who believed that Brown and his men were the victims of an unjust system, so the ceremony at the funeral was solemn. There were not many there, but the majority of those in attendance were members of the Raritan Bay Union, a society in Perth Amboy, for which Rebecca was a founding member.

Using the in-vogue European Transcendentalism model of a utopian society with the importance placed on education, music, classical literature, and thinking on a higher order, the Raritan Bay Union sought to establish a colony of freedom of expression and equality for all humans, established by the fact that all humans are interconnected, regardless of race or gender. She was raised a Quaker, so Rebecca lived a religious and regimented life.

Spring believed in the inherent goodness of people, and she saw that institutions and misguided values corrupted the individual, especially in America. This dose of American Transcendentalism tinged with Neo-European Romanticism with an understanding that evil must be combatted with evil created her and Brown's "by any means necessary" position. Spring and the Raritan Bay Union had the understanding to overlook the misdeeds of Brown or James Montgomery, Aaron Stevens, and a young Absalom Hazlett.

The Raritans gave Stevens and Hazlett a hero's send-off. They wrapped their caskets in the American flag and placed them in two separate 4-foot-deep graves.

Out on the Wire (March 30, 1860)

Many newspapers across the country ran the same blurb about the hangings. The news even spread across the pond to London, where slavery was abolished in 1833. So, on page 6 of *The Daily News*, the following roundup appeared:

> Stevens and Hazlett were hanged at Charlestown, Virginia, on the 16th, for their participation in the Harpers Ferry affair. Both men exhibited great firmness and resignation. There were no religious ceremonies at the gallows, as the prisoners persisted in refusing all the offices of the ministry in their last moments.[23]

4

William Harrison Faces Extradition

Placing the Defendant at the Scene of the Crime (February 8, 1860)[1]

Judge Richard Parker was visibly irate and irritated. He was short with the witnesses, but they all did what they were there to do—confirm the fact that Hazlett was at the scene of the crime and that he could be identified properly. The Jefferson County prosecutor, Charles Harding, dressed slovenly and put together a slovenly case.

He had a reputation of being a drunk, but this case on the surface looked like an easy slam dunk. The past two days had been unfruitful, though, and things were not coming together as easily as they should have for the home team. The proceedings that started at 10 o'clock that Wednesday morning had thus far not turned up anything worth noting.

Yesterday, Harding called a small parade of witnesses, including W. H. Harrison, George Samuel Collis, and other residents of Harpers Ferry, who testified that they could fully identify the defendant as being a participant at the invasion of the town. Harrison had the most details in his testimony, saying that Hazlett and another man, who he later found out to be Edwin Coppoc, were together and headed to the Rifle Factory. He said that he could see that Hazlett was carrying an easily identifiable Sharps rifle.

One of the star witnesses of the Cumberland County trial was called to the witness stand again during this trial. Mr. Copeland put Hazlett at the armory and implicated him through a description to the court. Harding took him through the details of what happened in Harpers Ferry and the way he came in contact with Hazlett, who tried to stand behind an alias, William Harrison.

In the cross-examination, the defense attacked his testimony. "Is it true that you had difficulty identifying the defendant at the jailhouse that he was being held for trial?"

"No, sir, I did not." Copeland replied.

"Before the Cumberland County courts, you stood behind your right to remain silent and did not answer the question as to not being able to identify my client."

"When I entered the jail, I saw that man there sitting on a stool when we entered the cell. He was wearing a beard then, but I remember seeing him sitting there looking out of the cell while sitting on a short stool."

"No more questions, your Honor," they said dismissing the witness.

Mr. W. Henser of Chambersburg also took the stand the day before and gave testimony that he helped in Hazlett's arrest. What was most captivating is the reason for the arrest. "We thought that he was actually Captain Cook," he told the court. "We had gotten word that he, too, was on the run."

That morning was much the same—testimony that seemed flimsy and easily poked through.

"The state wishes to call Colonel Clene to the stand," the prosecutor announced. Clene was an older man with a hard exterior but seemed soft and gentle with his hand in the air, saying "I swear," with a meek voice to the court vows.

"Can you, sir, identify the defendant?"

"Yes, sir, I can."

"How do you know him?"

"I had never met him before, and quite honestly, I cannot even tell you the gentleman's real name."

"Then, why are you hear, sir?"

"Well, sir, I first met the defendant in jail. We had a cordial conversation in which he casually mentions that he had not seen his mother since the Harpers Ferry affair. He was sad and lost in thought, but he seemed to instantly come to and regret his choice of words."

"Did you ask him to clarify what he said or meant by what he said?"

"No, sir, I did not." After a few more questions that seemed to fall flat, Colonel Clene was dismissed from the stand. At 4 p.m., the Commonwealth prosecutors said that they had completed their testimony and, "We rest our case, your Honor."

At the defense table, Lawson Botts and Thomas C. Green put their heads together, nodded in agreement, and then Green got up and went to work. Green was an enormous thirty-nine-year-old man, contrasting well against the thin lankiness of Lawson. He was tall and broad-shouldered, and his demeanor conveyed a sense of strength, confidence, and competence.

The first witness that the defense called to the stand was Major Armstead M. Ball. He was one of the hostages who was a chief witness during Brown's trial back in January. He was also one of the cornerstones for the prosecution of Hazlett. "Mr. Ball, the prosecution had you point out to the court that as the Master Machinist at the Arsenal you could see that there were four sentinels giving watch over the arsenal. Is that correct?"

"Yes, sir, it is," confirmed Ball.

"You said that you could identify two of these sentinels as Negroes, correct?"

"Yes, sir, that is correct. Two of them were Negroes. That was plain to see."

"Of the other two men, you can identify Mr. Coppoc, but you admit to having difficulty in identifying Mr. Hazlett, correct?" Green asked.

"Umm, that is correct." Ball said with hesitation.

"Major, could you take us through the incidents that happened the morning of August 16th, 1859?"

"Well, sir," Ball started. "Early that morning, I was made awake by Benjamin Hobbs, telling me that persons were at the Armory carrying off Government property. I quickly got dressed and reached the gate when I was accosted by two armed men and seized as a prisoner."

"When you were taken to the Armory yard as a prisoner, who stood watch?"

"Stevens was sentry at the gate. He then took me before John Brown."

"And what did Brown say to you?"

"He said that his 'object was to free the slaves and not the making of war on the people.' He said that my person and private property would be safe and that his was against the accursed system of slavery. He said that he had the power to do it and would carry it out. It was no child's play that he had undertaken." Ball readjusted himself in his chair.

"You testified then that he allowed you to go home to have your breakfast that you had missed in your haste, correct?" Green asked.

"Yes, sir, indeed he did," Ball confirmed. "He wanted to show his good faith, I suppose. He wanted me to return to my family, assure them that I would be safe, and then return as a matter of formality."

"You were escorted home by two men?"

"Yes, sir, I was. When we got to my house, my wife had not started breakfast, not knowing what awaited me when I got back to the Armory or knowing when I would return. So, the two men took me back to the armory. That is when Brown told me that it was his determination to seize the arms and munitions of the government, to arm the slaves to defend themselves against their masters."

"Did he send you back home to eat breakfast, like he promised?"

"Indeed, he did. Those same two men took me back," Ball said.

"The same two men? Are you sure?" Green walked to the judge's bench.

"Yes, sir, it was the same two men that served as my escort."

"The state asserts that one of these men was Mr. Coppoc and the other was the defendant, but you are unable to definitively testify to this fact, isn't that right, sir?"

"That is fact, sir," Ball affirmed.

"No more questions, your Honor."

Newspapers applauded the defense presented by Botts and Green, who called several other witnesses that were on Shenandoah Street during the raid, but none of them paid attention enough to later identify Hazlett standing guard on the street for the court.

The Nation Pays Attention as the Case Closes (February 10, 1860)

The interest in the trial grew the crowds, and now that it seemed like the case of Commonwealth *v.* Hazlett was drawing to a close, the courthouse was packed with people inside and outside on the courthouse lawn.

The two state prosecutors have been soundly criticized throughout history for presenting sloppy cases for the Commonwealth. These were important cases—Brown, Stevens, Hazlett, and the others captured and tried—and the question was if these two men could handle the pressure with such high stakes. Charles Harding was known to come to court inebriated, and it was not uncommon to see him fall asleep during testimony. His hair was as disheveled as his food-stained suits, and his questioning and remarks were just as out-of-sorts. Those who knew him well described him as such: "When Harding began to speak, if you shut your eyes and listened for the first few minutes, you would think Patrick Henry had returned to earth; after that he dwindled away into ineptitudes."[2]

Behind Harding's back, all correspondence started with Andrew Hunter. If Governor Wise or Judge Parker had a question or an issue, they started with Andrew Hunter, and it usually ended there, too. Hunter was the epitome of Southern gentility. He spoke eloquently, dressed handsomely, and conducted himself like a professional. However, he was quoted as saying, "Harding is a pestiferous little prosecutor," when asked about his partner.[3]

Hunter stood out during the Brown trial. He attacked with aggressiveness, met every counter with tact and strength, and demonstrated an efficiency that brought the swift justice that the townspeople were thirsting for. In the case of Stevens, it was Hunter who wrote to the judge and Governor Wise, "Stephens [*sic.*] will hardly be fit for trial. He will probably die of his wounds if we don't hang him promptly."[4]

At 9.30 on Friday morning, it was Harding who opened for the state, giving a ninety-minute closing argument. He came out swinging, but as charged, he lost steam by the end of a long, spiraling summation.

Lawson Botts, Esq., then took the court on a two-hour journey through the trial and the list of witnesses that could not identify Absalom Hazlett as any of his aliases—Edward Hazlett, Albert Hazlett, or William Harrison. Botts was from Fredericksburg, once studied at the Virginia Military Institute, and was appointed by the courts to defend Brown, so he had Hazlett's case. He was thin with high cheekbones, a closely cropped and manicured beard and mustache, and a long thin nose that looked like it may have once been broken in the past. He had deep-set and dark eyes with straight brows that made him look perpetually serious.

To those looking on at his dissection of the case and weak argument constructed by the prosecution, there was serious doubt as to which direction the jurors would lean. Botts was convincing. He said that the case presented against his client was fraught with discrepancies and built on circumstantial evidence. He pointed out how the witnesses were unsure of themselves, and their testimonies rang hollow and rehearsed. Yet the most damning element of the case left by the prosecutors was the nagging doubt of this being a case of mistaken identity:

> Ladies and gentlemen of the jury, I leave you with one last thought. I charge you with the duty to give my client the benefit of the doubt. The penalty for his crimes is death, so we must be sure we are sentencing the right man to condemnation.

Botts finished his statements at 1 o'clock, making strong appeals to the jury. It was a long, grueling morning. The judge wanted to skip lunch and push on, but sensing the fatigue of those in his court, he decided to take a half-hour recess instead of the full hour.

When they returned, Green made his closing arguments. It was a three-hour tirade that retried Brown's case, put the institution of slavery on trial, and made a mockery of this litigation that could not determine if it was Absalom Hazlett or another man named William Harrison being scapegoated. If this man was Hazlett, then it must be proved that he was at the scene of the crime. That was not done. If this man is, indeed, William Harrison, then there is absolutely no case brought against him, and the prosecution failed to confirm the defendant's identification beyond a shadow of a doubt.

Mr. Hunter closed the case for the prosecution, and he, too, set out a three-hour case for the conviction of the prisoner.

> Not only is there an overwhelmingly significant amount of eyewitness accounts of this man standing here before the court, being at the scene of the crime and armed with a Sharps rifle, regardless of his name, or what he claims it to be, or where he says he is from, we can put him there. Furthermore, we can suppose that he has either killed before or, at least, has taken part in other raids that terrorized innocent civilians. He is not,

nor will he ever be a martyr. He is a lowly, two-bit murderer who stands for cruelty, treason, and lawlessness. In leveling justice on this man, we will not promote his martyrdom. Instead, we will be righting a wrong.

We must convince these ruffians that what they are doing is wrong and punishable by death. We will not succumb to anarchy, wretchedness, and a conspiracy to undermine our institutions, our way of life, and the fabric that binds us together.

If you care at all about any of those things, ladies and gentlemen of the jury, then you must find this man guilty of the charges of murder, treason, and inciting slaves to rebellion. The state rests, your Honor.

The Verdict (February 11, 1860)

News was not printed in real time, like this recap that took ten days after the verdict was given to show up in *The Charlotte Democrat* on Tuesday the 21st. Editorializing was not an uncommon practice, so throughout the timeline of the trial in the newspaper, Hunter (the prosecutor for the Commonwealth) was characterized as being "one with much ability," while Mr. Green, who was fighting a losing battle, defended his client in the "best possible light" and his "effort was the ablest argument made since the commencement of the Harpers Ferry trials."[5]

> Saturday Morning—The jury came into court at half-past nine and the Clerk propounded the question whether they had agreed upon a verdict, to which the foreman responded they had. The prisoner was then sent for and brought into court. The verdict of the jury was then announced, which was "guilty of murder in the first degree." The prisoner received the verdict with the same indifference that has characterized his conduct, throughout the trial.[6]

The article ended with the following: "CHARLESTOWN, Feb. 15 – Stevens and Hazlett, the last of the Harpers Ferry outlaws, have been sentenced to be hanged on Friday, 16th of March. Both made speeches."[7] This southern paper chose not to run the speeches, like *The Carlisle American.*

A Penny Toss (February 12, 1860)

Stevens spent a total of 169 days in prison and Hazlett 150. Reporters and those at the jail were in awe of the coolness and an apparent acceptance that both had of their fate. They made friends and struck up a mutual respect with Captain Avis.

The very next day of their sentence, the two prisoners were embroiled in a competition of "chucking pennies" that got the attention of Avis. "No, No, No," Hazlett said. "Best two out of three."

"Okay," said Stevens, "this is the last toss then. Winner take all, the Grand Prize!" He hunched over and got ready to toss. He looked into the eyes of Hazlett. As the jailer looked on, Stevens flicked the coin; as it tossed flipping through the air, he called out, "Head or tail?"

"Tail!" shouted Hazlett.

There was a moment of suspense and Stevens walked over to examine the penny. He bent over to look at the penny and picked it up. "Ah, ha! It's head! I've won!" Hazlett slapped his knees in defeat.

Avis looking on, couldn't help but wonder, "What have you won?" he asked.

"The privilege of selecting you to put the hangman's noose around my neck!" was the cool reply.[5]

When Stevens stepped on the trap on the gallows that fateful day, he would remind Avis of this contest and its results. Onlookers saw the exchange, wondering what could have possibly transpired, but knew that in a few moments, only Avis would be able to tell the story.

Back to Ol' Virginny (February 22, 1860)

The Carlisle American ran a story summarizing Hazlett's long legal journey through the Cumberland County courts that extradited him back to Virginia. The article then went on to trace the happenings through to the trial that found him guilty of murder and inciting a slave rebellion. At no time did Hazlett ever implicate himself, or others for that matter, for taking part in the raid; instead, he charged prosecuting witnesses with perjury. Hazlett gave a statement to the local newspaper, and they printed his statement verbatim:

> I have a few words to say. I am innocent of the charge on which I have been convicted. I deny ever having committed murder of ever having contemplated murder, or ever having associated with anyone with such intentions. Some of the witnesses have sworn to things which I deny, and which were positively false. For instance, in reference to my beard; I have never in my life, until my imprisonment in jail, allowed my beard to go more than three weeks without shaving, and all testimony therefore as to the length of my beard is false. Again, Mr. Copeland testified that I was sitting on a stool when he entered the cell at Carlisle; this I deny. I was sitting on a blanket, back against the wall, and another man was on the stool. Copeland also said there were only two men in the cell; this is false, as there were four other white men in the cell with me.[9]

5

The Transition to Bondage

The Arrest (October 22, 1859)

Thanks to discrepancies in reporting, there is not one definitive account of the apprehension of Absalom Hazlett. Joseph D. Cress (in his article "Cumberland County's Connection to John Brown's Raid at Harpers Ferry") details the differences in the local newspaper accounts.

In the October 26 edition of *The Carlisle American*, it was said that the stranger was arrested with slight resistance, carrying four loaded revolvers, a Bowie knife, some little money, and an advertising circular for a book called *The History of Slavery.* The stranger, who called himself William Harrison, was described as 6 feet tall, well-built, with red hair and a thin, sandy beard. He was dressed in a red muslin shirt and dirty dark pants. As given the circumstances, he was a "rather hard-looking individual."[1]

By contrast, the rival newspaper in town, The *American Volunteer* had in its report that the man was taken into custody on West High Street with no resistance to arrest. Their October 27 article claimed that the man was armed with three revolvers and two Bowie knives. The paper went on to report that this William Harrison was brought before the district justice around noon on October 22 and refused to answer any questions, "saying only he was innocent and did not want a hearing at the time."[2]

In actuality, however, some historians suggest that Hazlett may have been unarmed, and this is what could account for him being so easily apprehended without a struggle. Since he could not be seen carrying a rifle going from town to town and he had little to no ammunition left, he ditched the Sharps rifle escaping over the wall at the boarding house in Chambersburg. As for the revolver, which is on display at the Kansas Historical Society in Topeka, Kansas, Hazlett was said to have traded his only weapon for a night's stay at an inn in Oakville, Pennsylvania. Yet, a revolver was said to have been in his possession, and Judge Watts was reported to be able to compare said revolver to those confiscated from the other raiders during their arrests.[3]

While Hazlett faced the District Justice (known as Squire Sponsler) that afternoon, an unassuming attorney, W. J. Shearer, was walking into town from his home on South Hanover Street to the courthouse. What first caught his attention was the unusual amount of people who had gathered outside of the courthouse, so he crossed the street and entered the building. There he found Bill Houser and Charlie Campbell of Chambersburg, two men who had been tracking the man they thought to be John Cook, along with a tall, raw-boned stranger seated nearby.[4] Approaching, Shearer asked, "What's going on here, gentlemen? What are you all doing?"

Houser replied, "Here is Cook, one of John Brown's men. He was in Chambersburg and slipped out, and came down here, and we followed him and arrested him up the railroad."[5]

"Which is Cook?" Shearer asked.

Houser and Campbell both pointed to the stranger, "Well, here he is right here."

"No, that cannot be Cook," Shearer started. "I have never seen Cook, but he is described as being an effeminate looking man with light hair and blue eyes. This is no such man."[6] He went over and pulled the man up by his shoulders. "This man is obviously a laborer. Look at his hands. Consider his build. This man does not match the descriptions of Cook." He tapped the stranger's shoulder and sat him back down.

"Well, quite frankly, I don't give a damn," Houser snapped back. "We are satisfied that he is one of John Brown's men. He was on the run, and now he is in our custody."

"But I am sure you are familiar with due process, correct? What do you plan to do with this man?"

Houser answered, "We're now drawing up the paperwork to extradite this man back to Charlestown to stand trial."

"Back to Charlestown?" Shearer shot back. "He was captured here. At the very least, shouldn't he be tried here? But ultimately, given that the alleged crime was against a federal armory, shouldn't he be tried in the federal courts?" Shearer turned his attention to the man that sat there unassumingly, not saying a word, not eliciting any type of reaction. "Sir," he said, "do you know of any attorneys in Carlisle that might represent you?"

"I do not, sir. My name is William Harrison, and I am here originally from Indiana County. I do not know of any attorneys from this county," he said. "Will you see that I have justice done me?"[7]

"I will agree to look over the extradition hearing of the Cumberland County Court, but I cannot yet agree to anything more." Immediately, he turned on Sponsler. "My first official act as this man's attorney, I must warn you that you have no right to draw papers on sending Mr. Harrison, a resident of this Commonwealth, back to Virginia without proper court approval."

"A hearing!" Houser yelled. "There will be no hearing. This man is going back to Charlestown and face the fear and terror that he caused that poor town."

"No, sir, Harrison will be staying," he calmly said.

"You, sir, are out of line! I am, personally, taking this man back to Virginia!"

Shearer replied, "I don't believe you will."[8] He raised a finger, as if to say, wait there just one moment, and walked over to the door, opened it, and called out. "Sheriff McCartney?" He paused and called again, "Sheriff McCartney? May I have a word with you please?"

Sheriff McCartney entered the room with his deputy shadowing him. "Sheriff, I ask you to stand outside of this office, and arrest these two gentlemen, Houser and Campbell, on kidnapping charges if they dare attempt to leave this office with this man." The sheriff unwillingly nodded and left the room to his post. Shearer turned back to Houser. "Now, sir, you asserted that you were taking this man to Virginia, and I said, 'I don't believe you will.' Are you going to continue to insist upon taking this man out of this office until he is given a proper hearing?"

"I guess not," Houser conceded.[9]

The Writ of *Habeas Corpus* (October 23–26, 1859)

Shearer recruited William H. Miller and Alexander Sharp as the defense team. They filed a writ of *habeas corpus* on behalf of William Harrison before county court. The first hearing of the writ was four days later before Judge James H. Graham. Representing the interests of the state of Virginia was council Judge Frederick Watts of Cumberland County Pennsylvania.

Judge Watts with his identifiable mutton-chop sideburns had a long career in law and agriculture. He later went on to establish "The Farmers High School" that grew to become Penn State University. Judge Watts presented a warrant from Pennsylvania Governor William Packer requesting the release of Albert Hazlett to Virginia authorities.[10] Watts also made the connection between the revolvers used by the raiders at Harpers Ferry. He pointed out that the revolvers found on the stranger were the same make and model as those used by Brown and the others. It was also noted that witnesses described a man who matched Harrison's description was seen at the scene of the insurrection.

Judge Graham was unimpressed with the arguments and was not convinced that the right thing to do was send this stranger back to Virginia without speaking with some of the witnesses. He gave Watts three days, which would be Saturday, October 29, to round up the witnesses from Harpers Ferry and get them to Cumberland County.

"Sheriff, That Is My Man!" (October 29–November 5, 1859)

The second hearing commenced, and Watts was able to get a number of Harpers Ferry residents to testify. One, a Mr. Collis, said he and a neighbor talked to the man in custody in the street and had examined his rifle to see if it was loaded. They thought the prisoner was a member of a volunteer militia on his way to the Winchester Fair. That presumption changed when two other men, armed the same way, forced Collis, his neighbor, and a third man to march to the armory as prisoners.[11]

A second witness took the stand, Mr. Copeland. He said, "I saw that man there discharge his rifle at about the same time I saw a fellow resident fall dead in the street."

"Was he aiming and shooting to kill that individual?" Shearer asked.

"Well, I cannot say for sure. From where I was standing, I could see the muzzle flash, but I am not 100 percent sure if that man there was definitively the one who killed the man. I couldn't tell exactly where he was aiming, but the gun went off, and the man fell in succession like that."

"Like Mr. Collis, you swore to the identity of the prisoner here in this courtroom, yet you failed to recognize him earlier while visiting the county jail. What is your explanation for that, Mr. Copeland?"

"What do you mean?" Mr. Copeland asked in confusion.

"You see, Mr. Copeland," started Shearer, "I had arranged with Sheriff McCartney to take you to different cells if you asked to see the prisoner that you were to testify against. So lo and behold, the first thing that you, Mr. Collis, and witness number three did when you got to town is go to the jail and ask Sheriff McCartney to see the defendant. Instead of taking you to the cell of Mr. Harrison, the sheriff took you to another's cell. Now, you can easily identify the prisoner, but earlier you, nor any of you, could identify if that man was or was not at the scene of the crime. Is that true, Mr. Copeland?"

"I ... well ... I ..."

"Yes or no, sir, please. It is a simple yes or no question. Did you have trouble identifying the prisoner at the jailhouse?"

"Sir, I plead the fifth. I have been instructed to not say anything about what happened at the jail."

The days' work of the witnesses and county prosecutors produced negative results. *The Carlisle American* questioned the integrity of those giving testimony. Of the one witness account that saw the prisoner not only shoot at citizens but saw the man patrol the town streets armed with a gun as he "stood sentinel at the armory. Whether they testified truthfully," they wrote, "we leave to everyone to form their own opinion."[12] The paper also went on to show discrepancies in witness testimony. For example, one witness saw him dressed in a red flannel jacket with pockets on the side, while another said they saw him wearing a striped shirt with a dark slouch hat.[13]

Through it all, Watts stood firm on his position that he could put Harrison at the scene of the crime, and that was enough proof to send him to Charlestown, Virginia, to be tried. Watts pressed Graham on the fact that the Colt revolvers, regardless of the amount found on his person, were of the kind found also on the other insurgents.

The defense team, led by Shearer, asserted that those wanting to extradite the man in custody did not give sufficient evidence to even identify the man, undoubtedly, as Absalom "Albert" Hazlett. He, therefore, asked the judge to either dismiss this case, set Harrison free, or to put him in custody of the sheriff until his identification can, indeed, be confirmed.

Tormented by the need to give a decision and the ethical need to get it right, Judge Graham passed down the decision that they would take some time to gather more evidence and definitively identify the prisoner being held. A third hearing was scheduled for November 5.

Shearer wrote a paper published by the Hamilton Library Association in 1905, where he documented two separate occasions in which he protected the man he represented with the help of Sheriff McCartney.

In one instance, Shearer got information that the witnesses had arrived at Carlisle, and right away, he went to the sheriff and asked, "Have the witnesses been to the jail yet?"

"No, sir, they haven't," answered McCartney. "They are over there at the hotel smoking their breakfast cigars and then they are coming over."[14]

"Okay, then. You are the sheriff. It is your business to keep the prisoner, and not to deliver him to anyone unless they identify him. I am this man's counsel and I warn you not to spot him. You have no right to pick him out for them. If they want him, they ought to know him."

"I understand," agreed the sheriff.

"I ask that you set all 100 inmates loose inside the main corridor and let them pick him out."[15]

As asked, when the men arrived after finishing their after-breakfast cigars, one of them asked, "So, out of all of these men, which one is Hazlett?"

"Take a look for yourself," McCartney said. "You ought to know the man. Look in there, he is there."[16]

The men grumbled and looked over the prisoners in the main corridor. They gave stern looks at the sheriff and whispered among themselves. Eventually, they left the jail frustrated. They admitted to one another as they were exiting the building that they could not identify the man who called himself William Harrison.

On the second occasion, the next group was more confident that they could identify the prisoner, so Shearer had a different strategy. "Sheriff, do you have a man who you know to fit the description of my counselee?"

"I know of just the man," he answered.

"Good. Have that man exchange clothes and sit in the same cell together. This imposter will avoid contact with the witnesses. He will look to the floor and hang his head as in guilt. Hazlett on the other hand will keep his head high and look the witnesses in the eye."

When the witnesses arrived, they looked at the actor and said, "Sheriff, that is my man."[17]

"You must be mistaken, sirs. That man was born and reared in Carlisle, and has never been out of Carlisle," McCartney corrected.

By the time the third trial was heard, all of the paperwork was properly patched up in that all names—William Harrison, Elbert Hazlett, and Albert Hazlett—were added to the warrant. The agent appointed by Virginia was William N. Kelly, and by the end of the hearing, it was determined that the prisoner had to be turned over to him to be taken to Charlestown.

Judge Watts' final ruling said, "There is no evidence that we have any man in our custody named Albert Hazlett, we are satisfied that a monstrous crime has been committed and the prisoner ... participated in it."[18]

That afternoon, Hazlett was put on a train while a "considerable crowd expressing a great deal of sympathy" followed the prisoner "from the jail to the train," as *The Carlisle American* reported.[19] Hazlett, while he walked to board the train, denounced the proceedings and maintained his innocence.

Agitated and frustrated by the legal actions, the students of nearby Dickinson College staged a demonstration and protested the decision with bonfires, chants in the streets, and unruly conduct that disrupted the entire town. Residents wrote letters to the editors of both local newspapers decrying the students' behavior, but that only seemed to ensure that the students would keep up the protests for a few extra days.

6

Life, Liberty, and the Pursuit of Absalom Hazlett

On the Run (October 19–22, 1859)

For about three hours, Absalom Hazlett and Osborne Anderson took turns taking little naps. The raid had failed, and they had watched from the United States Armory and Arsenal at Harpers Ferry complex building window as Brown's fort was overtaken by the militia. The mission was over, so they retreated to cover in the mountains. For a period, they talked and speculated a little about plans of action, outcomes of their fellow raiders and possible survivors, and pathways that they could take back to home base, the Kennedy farm, or the schoolhouse, or if need be Canada, Osborne's homeland. Then when darkness was about to fall and there was a solid hour or so of complete quiet, Hazlett and Anderson made their way back down the mountainside to circle to the backside of the town.

Before darkness fell, they heard voices emerging from the woods and into a small clearing where sediment rock made coverage impossible. A small band of uniformed men was in pursuit and trying to fan out to push to the steep incline. Hazlett and Anderson sat in their birds' nest and dropped a handful of Lee's men with their sharpshooter skills that they honed with training at the farm. They were as calm and at ease as if it were target practice. The small search party recognized right away that they were outflanked, even though they had the advantage of numbers, and so they were forced back into the safety of the woods.

Lack of ammo was the second mistake the two had seen made since Brown ordered the train to be allowed to make its way to the authorities in Baltimore. There were other critical errors committed by the band that foiled the mission, but all they could do was move forward and find a way to survive. Due to the little melee, the duo was dangerously low on ammunition. To make matters worse, they realized that they had not had anything to eat for about two days. They were able to keep their empty gnawing of hunger out of mind with the concentration that it took to escape the Arsenal, to run the tracks to the Shenandoah with a hostage, to fight off a small band of troops, and to make it this far back to the Virginia side of the Ferry just to stay alive and have the opportunity to be on the run.

When they descended the crag and entered the town once again, they noticed that the man that they took hostage crossing the railroad tracks was right—order was, indeed, restored in the town, so much so, that an eerie quiet pervaded that was even more soundless than before they had first ascended on the town in the predawn hours. The ferry had deserved its rest, and it never would have expected any of the raiders to dare make their way back into the town. Yet Hazlett and Anderson were stealing a boat under the cover of night, and they began to quietly and measuredly paddle toward the banks of Maryland on the Potomac River.

The walk back to the farm was about 5 miles, depending on how straight they could make their path, and the skies were heavy with rain and moisture as the temperature noticeably began to drop. Once they made it to the Maryland side, they passed "along the two-path of the canal for some distance" and got to an arch that directed its way back to the farm.[1] They treaded their way north, expecting to meet back up with Owen Brown, F. J. Merriam, and Barclay Coppoc stationed as lookouts and protectors of their food and belongings, but when they reached the farm, their hopes of gaining provisions for a long course to freedom were dashed. The farmhouse was deserted, ransacked, and stripped of anything of value. They turned their attentions on making it to the schoolhouse, where surplus was stored for just such an occasion. The schoolhouse was also part of phase two of the plan, for the three on guard at the farmhouse were to wait for others and transport arms and supplies to the schoolhouse.

At about 2 o'clock that morning, they had not yet made it as far at the schoolhouse, and after crossing back through the mountains and reaching the flatlands, they were not that far from the Ferry. It was about a ninety-minute hike from the farmhouse, and the rain once again began to heavily fall. They were wet and exhausted. "I'm too tired to push on tonight, and my feet are killing me," Hazlett said. "Let's just hide out here until morning."

"It's unsafe here," said Anderson. "With how tired we both are, there's a chance we'll sleep in and be sitting ducks. Let's push on and get position in the mountains instead."

Hazlett thought about it, knew that Anderson was right, and agreed to go a little further into the mountains that stood behind the schoolhouse. They rested easily—so easily, in fact, that the rain had lifted, the sun was up, and gunshots could be heard coming from the Ferry.

"That has to be Owen and his men," Hazlett said. "That's why there wasn't anyone left at the farmhouse. They must've gotten word that the Captain had been taken prisoner, and they are attempting to rescue him and shoot their way out." The two set out down the ridge to help in the fight. They made it back to the Ferry and saw that the troops were firing toward the Maryland side across the river. They followed the militia's aim with their eyes and saw the targets—slaves that Brown's men had equipped with pikes the day before.[2] These rebel slaves were originally posted up at the schoolhouse by Tidd, and now they were flushed out and had retreated into the bushes at the foot of the mountain cut out by the river.

Knowing that they had the advantage of gunpower, the troops gave chase across the bridge, and the slaves scattered and hid. There was a random shot here and there, and from their lookout, they could see the troops regather at the bridge and walk back over into the Ferry. Waiting in their hiding spot for any more signs of activity, one of the slaves now on the run came within yards of them. He was oblivious to their presence. "Psst," they called to him to get his attention without scaring him. "Psst!"

"Who dare?" the man said, raising his pike with fear and trepidation.

"Brown's men," Hazlett said in hushed tones. That name carried great weight among slaves. They called the man to them and Anderson made himself visible. The man approached them. "What were you guys doing?" Hazlett asked. "There has been nothing but mayhem in the streets. I can't believe you didn't hear the commotion. You didn't hear Captain Brown was holed up in the Engine House, and he was either killed or captured by the militia? What brought you here at this time?"

"We knowed yous in the Ferry. We come to fight, suh," he answered.

In a series of mistakes and missteps, it was clear that a better-coordinated effort was called for. After giving the pikes to the slaves who had the courage to rebel, better instructions for them could have improved their timing and saved lives. "Were any of your men killed?"

"Yessuh," he confirmed. "A good man named Joe. He was shot and is lying there on the ground." Albert and Osborne began scanning the foot of the mountain to see if the man could be spotted. The refugee pointed in a specific direction, and just a little bit of the victim's blue shirt could be spotted through the bushes and brush that bearded the mouth of the river and the incline of the mountain.

"What is your name?" Osborne asked.

"Homer Edgefield, suh."

"We are headed back to the schoolhouse to get some supplies and hopefully meet up with some of the others," said Osborne. "Why don't you come with us?"

"No, suh, Ise got a wife and kids I mus' tend to. I'se lef the schoolhuss. It not safe dare."

"It's not safe by yourself. What if you get caught? Your kids will have a dead father," Albert said in almost a snarl. "Your wife will be a widow."

"I tooks dat chance when da pike wah put in mah hands," he responded.

"Look," said Osborne. "Our main goal is freedom. You can come with me to Canada. You will have a chance to come back and buy your family's freedom."

The slave thought a bit, and then a few moments more. It was clear that he was processing the notion but could not wrap his head around the concept of freedom. "Nossuh, I be goin back."

"Well, good luck," Osborne said.

"Thank you, suh," Homer responded. He looked to Albert.

Albert nodded in frustration and turned away from the man without saying anything. "I don't understand it," he said with his back turned, intending only Osborne to hear.

Homer went off into the cover of the trees. He climbed the steepness of the mountain with his feet out turned and his hands hovering the earth for stability and agility. Quickly he was gone in the direction he was headed before being flagged down.

Albert and Osborne made their way to a perch so that they could observe any activity at the schoolhouse, instead of just blindly approaching it. Lo and behold, their patience paid off. A troop of soldiers were securing the area before entering and taking it. The two watched it all play out, knowing that their chances of any type of meal were dashed. They knew that if any of the three men were inside, they were taken peacefully, for there were no shots fired after entry.

Hazlett and Osborne stayed hidden in the cradle of the wooded hillside and watched. A couple of wagons came and stopped outside, and the soldiers began loading crates onto them. It did not take long before they cleared what they wanted and began heading back into town. The two kicked back and deeply exhaled. It was a sigh but not one of relief. "It really is just us now," Albert said.

"Yep," Osborne agreed.

"What is the plan now? What do we do?"

"It's like I told Homer. We can go on to Canada to our freedom," Osborne said, half-stating and half-asking.

"Well," said Albert, "without question we do head north, but as far as Canada, I don't know."

They got up, brushed themselves off, rolled their blankets, and started in a northern direction. They were famished, and with the amount of energy exerted to this point, though most of it was running on adrenaline, their muscles were greatly fatigued and cramped. Their bodies ached, and descending the hills took as much exertion as climbing them, though the more they walked, the more the landscape started to level off and roll more gently.

Another mountain range was within sight, and darkness was not too far off. They figured that if they could find a cornfield to scavenge some ears, they could hide up in the mountain, eat, rest, and start fresh in the morning. Once they found a cornfield, they went into the mountains to search for a spot to set up a camp with good cover. They located a spot and gathered some wood, and when it was dark enough, they went into the field and filled their arms and pockets with corn. They returned, and Albert started a fire with one of the few matches that he happened to have left. With the fire started, they began roasting their corn, and though it was fall-hardened and tough, they "roasted and feasted."[3]

What they did not eat, they kept as leftovers that they took with them when they resumed their journey north in the morning. Being tall, thin, and lanky is not the proper body type to send through dense forest that battles with streams, topography, fallen trees, sharp brier patches, and the unexpected. It was not that Albert was unathletic; it was the simple fact that each step brought a persistent pain from his blistered feet and because the corn was giving no sustenance and was running right through him because his body was rejecting, instead of taking in and nourishing.

Osborne, on the other hand, was much more used to extended periods of strenuous, physical activity. He never pushed Albert, though he did encourage. When Albert would ask to stop for a break, Osborne would say, "Let's just get to the crest of the hill," or "there's a big group of trees on the top of that hill, so let's try to make it over to there."

It was probably around mid-afternoon when they crossed the Pennsylvania state line. Albert was about to quit there. Each step shot alarming pain from the blisters that broke and exposed raw skin. "We are about 20 miles to Chambersburg," Osborne coaxed. "You don't think you can make it there? I will leave you at the boarding house where Cook and Kagi stayed. You can eat and get some sleep, and then we join up again and keep pushing north."

"No, I won't be able to make it there today," Albert said collapsed on the ground. "Please, go on. I will rest and finish the trip into Chambersburg. If I find the right people there, I will be able to hide out for a while before going any further north. Canada is your ultimate goal anyway, so you might as well keep going. I would never make it that far. I had no intentions on going that far."

"I don't want to leave you out here in this condition," Osborne was almost pleading. "I want to see you settled at the boarding house."

Albert considered his options, took a few deep breaths, and then hauled himself up to his feet. It would be a well-deserved gift to lay in a bed and rest, instead of another night on the wet blanket that was a pillow, bedroll, and knapsack rolled into one. The wet and heavy shawl did more to weigh him down on his back during travel than give comfort during sleep. "I guess," he sighed, "if we push through, we should make it there by midnight. I will try to make it 'til then."

Travel was slow, much slower than expected or needed if they intended to make it to Chambersburg by midnight. They made as much time as they could by following what roads, trails, and railroad tracks that gave the easiest passage, but they stopped regularly for Hazlett to nurse his wounded feet.

Each step had to be carefully thought out, and Hazlett was so fatigued and muscle-spent that even motor functions did not come naturally. His mind tried picking up the slack, but even that was giving out. He caved in to the pain, fell to the ground, and welled up with tears in his eyes. "I'm not going to make it," he cried.

"We are only about 10 miles from our destination. Sure, we are behind, and it will be well after midnight, but there will be an end to it."

"Please," Albert said, "it is not even safe for you to travel with me in my condition. It is not safe for you to be seen with me in any condition because I am certain there are warrants out for us. Go on. Leave me here and go on to Chambersburg."

"When will we meet again?"

"I must rest tonight," he emphasized. "In the morning, I'll throw away the rifle and flag down a farmer on his way to town. We can meet up then and decide what our next move should be."

Osborne helped Hazlett up to his feet and embraced him, and Albert cowered into a sob. "Good luck, my friend. We will meet in Chambersburg. I will try to send word for you at the boarding house." Osborne encouraged.

"I will be there," Albert confirmed.

Osborne held Albert's hand to steady him as he settled back on to the ground. It was dark, and the cold, crisp air called for a fire; therefore, Osborne cleared him out a space for a fire, gathered some wood with some large, dry pieces to throw on to last through the night, started the fire, and stayed until the red coals made a fast extinguish impossible.

After a while, Osborne got up to leave, and they said their goodbyes once again. Though he did not sob like he did earlier, there were tears in Albert's eyes as he was left alone. In an instant, Osborne stepped out of the light of the fire and into the darkness.

Albert woke to the call of a crow. The fire had reduced to gray ash and little puffs of smoke by morning because Albert never got up to throw any of the thick pieces on the fire that Osborne had set beside him. His mode of travel was just a bit more than a hobble, and he navigated his way to the Cumberland Valley Railroad tracks, which headed directly into Chambersburg. While walking along the tracks and still with his rifle wrapped in the shawl, a gentle old man in a horse and buggy was passing. "I see ya struggling along there, mister, would you like a ride?"

"Yeah, sure, that'll be great. Are you headed into Chambersburg?"

"No, not quite that far. I'll be branching off to head into Quincy; that's where I live, but I can drop you off right outside of town. That'll save you a lot of walking, which it looks like you're struggling with," the old man said. Even through the overgrown hair of his wiry, white mustache, it was clear that he was smiling.

"I greatly appreciate it," Albert said while stepping up into the buggy with the help of the man. Though the man was old, he had thick shoulders that tapered down to a thin stomach and waist. He wore an overcoat that was too large because the size was needed for his shoulders. He had a thin head of hair, well-manicured as was his sideburns and shaved cheeks and jawlines, but his goatee popped out on his chin and was feral and unkempt. Straggly, stringy white hairs reached all the way to his collar bone.

While they road along, they made small talk to pass some of the time. The man offered Albert some apples along with some dried meat and biscuits, and he accepted and ate all that the man was willing to give. They talked about superficial things like the weather, this past summer's growing season and harvest, and current events weighing on the country. "Have you heard about the incident down in Harpers Ferry?" Albert asked.

"Oh, sure," the old man said. "Everyone by now's heard about it."

"What do you think about it?"

"I think these are strange times we are living in," the old man said. "Why do you ask? What do you think about it?" His hawkish features were accentuated by a devious smile that Albert did not know how to interpret.

"I was just wondering," Hazlett said. "I think those men must've been crazy to try and pull something like that off in that crevice called Harpers Ferry," he answered in all honesty.

"Crazy. Yes," the old man agreed. "There's sign bills out advertising for the arrests of those who they know escaped." He sighed and nodded. There was a long pause of silence as the steady clip-clop of the horse's measured beat filled time and space. After some time, the old man asked, "I didn't get your name there, stranger. Whatta they call you?"

"Oh, I'm sorry. All this time with you and your graciousness, I didn't tell you my name. How rude. My name is William Harrison. And yours?"

"Hiram Wertz. Nice to meet you." They rode along until they came to a fork in the road, and the old man said, "Well, unless you want to come along with me, this is the road that branches off to Quincy. It's a nice quiet little town, if you want to visit. Otherwise, Chambersburg is about 3 miles if you follow this trail."

"No, thank you, sir. My business requires me to take another road.[4] I have family waiting for me in Chambersburg. They will wonder what happened to me if I don't make it into town today."

"Well, Mr. Harrison, it was nice meeting and talking to you. You sure helped pass some time. You know it gets lonely out there traveling."

"Yes, I know, sir. Thank you for the ride, Mr. Wertz. I will make it to Chambersburg in good time to meet up with my people there."

"Well, if you ever make it into Quincy," Wertz started. "Look me up. I have a farm there, so there's always work."

"That is very kind of you, sir. I may take you up on your offer some day," he said stepping down. The buggy veered off to the right and the pathway seemed much rougher than what they rode. Albert watched on as it dipped and dived in and out of holes in the road, throwing puddled water with each dip. Hazlett walked on, and though he was not picked up again, a shot of positivity and excitement confirmed that he would make it to town, meet up with Osborne, and reach safety further north.

It is worth noting here who Hiram Wertz was and the ironic implications of his offer to go on to Quincy. For at least fourteen years before Wertz met Absalom to give him a ride and leave him outside of Chambersburg, Wertz was a prominent conductor on the Underground Railroad. Through this part of Pennsylvania pre-Civil War, the Underground Railroad dotted along a path of iron furnaces and coal mining company towns. Crossing the Pennsylvania border, runaway slaves were put into the hands of Jacob Shockey, who owned a farm along the well-worn Indian trail that ran the South Mountain to eventually split off west to Waynesboro and Mercersburg, or northwest to Quincy.

Shockey would take the fugitives to Wertz in Quincy, a small hamlet about 3 miles north of the much larger Waynesboro, and the next phase in the escape route began with Wertz guiding the freedom seekers 8 miles northward to the small black community known as "Africa."[5]

Later in life, Wertz wrote extensively about his involvement in the Underground Railroad, and he even once mentioned how he "forever regretted that his hitchhiker never revealed his true mission" that day he and Hazlett crossed paths.[6]

Though Absalom ached, the walk was not quite as bad as it had been trying to keep pace with Osborne. He walked the 3 miles into town and made his way to the boarding house.

Abram Ritner was the proprietor of the boarding house, and he was involved in the abolitionist movement for years. He opened the boarding house to runaway slaves, and it is suspected by historians that he knew what John Brown was up to when he, Kagi, and Cook and others would stay there, leave, and return in intervals. Cook's wife, Virginia, and their baby lived there, so Albert assumed that he could rest, eat, and get news of what his next moves should be.

As not to raise suspicion, Hazlett walked nonchalantly in through the southern part of town, to Main Street, the heart of town, and to the west end of town to the two-story, three-bay-wide structure, known as the Ritner House. He entered the hewn-log building that was clapboard covered, and he walked down the hall to where he knew the Cooks stayed. He lightly knocked on the door, and Virginia answered.

She grabbed him and quickly pulled him inside. "What are you doing here?" She scolded.

"I am all by myself. I don't know what else more to do," he pushed back his emotions, composed himself, and continued speaking. "I don't have any idea of where to go or who to turn to. I was hoping that I could seek some sort of solace here."

"This place is being surveilled. There are signs posted all around for your arrests. It is not safe here. You must leave at once." It was an order and not a suggestion.

"What about the others?"

"It is over, Al. Over. It is every man for himself now." She spoke quickly and directly. "I have a small babe to care for. If I am questioned, I must own up to my husband, but I don't know the rest of you. Please. Leave at once. Please. Don't cause anyone else any more trouble. If you make it to freedom, and all else works out, we will meet again and talk, but right now, I don't know you and you must leave."

Just then, there was a knock on the door. Both knew who it was—bounty hunters. Virginia hurriedly pushed Albert to the back bedroom, said, "Leave," and closed the door. When he heard muffled voices in the front, he jumped out the back window, ran down the alley, doubled-back to the main street, caught back up to the Cumberland Valley tracks, and started up north toward Newville, making Carlisle the next destination.

As it turned out, the bounty hunters saw Hazlett early on when he first entered town. As innocuous as he intended to appear, he immediately caught the eye of the men by the Sharps rifle wrapped in a blanket that he was carrying under his arm. They had never heard of Absalom Hazlett, so they thought that he was the now infamous Captain James E. Cook, whose wanted sign was widely distributed and plastered in every

Dry Goods store and tavern in the surrounding areas. Going straight to the Ritner House automatically confirmed their suspicions that it was, indeed, Cook.

As for Virginia, she was later questioned and interrogated by bounty hunters, officials, and even a reporter from the local paper, *The Valley Spirit*. Her mother and younger brother were also put on the hot seat and interrogated. When news broke of the failed attempt at Harpers Ferry and the price on her husband's head, she hysterically wanted to leave the boarding house and visit her mother in Harpers Ferry. She made a couple attempts, calling herself "Miss Kennedy," but one time she was prevented by a stage driver who recognized her and said that he would not take her because she would never "get through alive."[7] At another time, she was stopped by her boarding mates and reminded that her baby needed her and that too much drunken excitement and violence was taking place in the Ferry.

During intense interrogations, she did not know much information, but she gave what she did know. She even made a startling personal revelation. All the questioning broke her down to embarrassingly admitting that she had lied on her baby's birth certificate, changing the date to make it appear that the baby was born in wedlock.[8] She was broken and left alone.

Thinking that the person making the visit to Ritner Boarding House was James Cook, it made no sense to authorities when they found a Sharps rifle wrapped in a blanket embroidered with the initials "E. H." The strange find was laying in the yard right on the other side of the fence that was scaled for the getaway. The suspect was followed by Bill Houser and Charlie Campbell, two bounty hunters from Chambersburg.

Those were the two that spotted Hazlett as he entered town. They kept their distance, and as Hazlett nonchalantly approached from the tracks to the Ritner House, Houser and Campbell nonchalantly followed. When Hazlett went inside the boarding house, the two plotted their capture. Houser waited out front while Campbell ran and got the sheriff for assistance. When they arrived, the sheriff went inside. Campbell positioned himself in the alleyway, while Houser stood at the front door, and the sheriff went to knock at the door. Campbell heard the clamoring of Hazlett going over the fence, but by the time he got there, the suspect was out of sight. Not of age or fitness to climb any fence, the two bounty hunters and the sheriff went the long way around to the other side of the fence to investigate. There in the grass, they found the rifle. Pressing themselves onto Mrs. Cook and a search of the flat returned no clues or positive results. Quickly deducing the pathway to freedom, the two bounty hunters gave chase. They bet on the Cumberland Valley tracks and followed those north.

The Last Days of Freedom (October 21 and 22, 1859)

Back on the run and really not clear as to what he should do, Albert defaulted to the most obvious impulse to keep trudging north. While he walked, he counted the days on the run to the day of the raid and figured the day to be Friday, October 21. He had not really thought about the passage of time, more focused on calculating the steps to freedom instead. Day and night ran together because his sleep pattern did not coincide with those natural parameters, ever since cultivating a nocturnal life at Kennedy Farm. From the start of the raid, natural order and any observance or perception of time were obliterated.

When he reached the town of Oakville, he was spent for the day, so he found a tavern with rooms upstairs. It was being run by a man named Robert Smith. He went into the tavern and went up to the bar. "Is the proprietor of this fine establishment available?" He asked the man behind the bar.

"This's him," the man said. He was a short, stout man with a large mustache, completely bald on top with short hair around the sides.

"I need a room for the night," Albert said. "However, I don't think I have enough money to cover it." He hesitated then asked, "Is there somewhere we could speak in private?"

He motioned Albert to the end of the bar. At the end of the bar was a small office; Smith went in and nodded for Albert to follow him. Once inside, he leaned over and inquired, "Now, whatcha talkin' bout?"

"I am short on cash, but I have this Colt revolver here that would undoubtedly cover the cost of a good night's sleep," he proposed.

He handed Smith the pistol. He looked it over on both sides, down the hammer and barrel, and said, "Yeah, this should do it. What's the name?"

"Harrison," Albert said. "William Harrison. I am on my way to visit family in Carlisle. I ran out of money and energy before I could make it. I'm coming from Indiana, Pennsylvania. I am close, aren't I?"

"Yeah, you're gettin' there," Smith said without any real sense of caring. He tucked the revolver away in a desk and pulled a key off a ring of others to give to Albert. "Drop the key off in the morning. If I'm not around, I'm busy elsewhere; leave it on the bar in there. Your room is upstairs, the first door on your left."

Albert climbed the stairs, opened his room, kicked off his boots, and plopped face-first into the bed. When he woke up at the very first crack of dawn, he was still in the same position. He had slept like a rock. He got up, brushed out the bed covers to how it was before dropping in it, and went downstairs to look for the innkeeper of the tavern. He was not around, so as instructed, Albert left the key in the middle of the bar.

He walked out the door and headed for the Cumberland Valley tracks that would take him to Carlisle.

The rain of the past few days was lifted, but the heavy overcast made everything seem wet and cold. His feet still hurt, but they were much improved. Raw skin was exposed from the popped blisters; however, he was able to alleviate all of the rubbing and aid in keeping them dry by laying a little paper into the instep and front bottom of the boot. The boots were tighter but more comfortable for walking because they no longer rubbed.

A few miles outside of Carlisle, the bounty hunters were not sure if they had overrun their assailant because they had pressed the search almost all night. Assuredly, the man thought to be Cook did not bypass them and make it into Carlisle, so they waited.

Sure enough, entering from the west end of the town of Newville was the man that they had seen entering the Ritner House wearing a red muslin shirt. This time, Houser went up further on a side street intersecting West High Street, the apparent destination. Campbell would then make himself seen and push Hazlett to Houser.

Hazlett saw Campbell right away. He began walking a little faster, though resisting the temptation to run as not to totally blow his cover. He peeked over his shoulder as he was about to make a left off West High Street. It was then that Houser appeared with his pistol drawn. "Going somewhere, Captain Cook?" he said.

"Captain Cook? You are mistaken, sir. My name is William Harrison. I am going into Carlisle to visit family."

"Like hell you are," Houser said. "Come with me. Won't be any trouble."

"No, sir, there won't be any trouble, as there shouldn't be. I think you will realize that you are making a mistake."

"Have any guns on ya?" He said, grabbing Albert and bending his arm behind his back. Campbell approached and grabbed the other arm. "Tell me!" He said with added infliction and volume.

"I am unarmed, sir. I know not this Captain Cook of whom you are referring."

"Oh, that's what they said. You fit the description all right." Campbell said laughing. "A pretty boy that talks all fancy."

Hazlett did not resist arrest, but that was not reason enough for Houser and Campbell to not rough him up and take turns dishing out cheap shots to the face and a few swift kicks as their victim fell and balled up in the fetal position to protect himself in the middle of the street. Though people went about their business, the scene did not go unnoticed.

Newspapers were not sure how to report this incident, so added details and varying specifics altered with each retelling of the narrative.

7

Personal Salvation

Three Days in Harpers Ferry (October 16, 17, and 18, 1859)

It was clear that no more men were coming to Kennedy Farm. John Brown, Jr.—though he was mentally scarred and not up to the task from the horrifying Pottawatomie episode in Kansas—traveled the eastern states and up through to Canada recruiting for his father, but he found no more men willing to go along with the plan to seize the Arsenal in Harpers Ferry. Some were counted on, like George Gill, Richard Richardson, and others who had stuck with Brown and proven themselves loyal to liberation, but even they never showed up to join the raiders as expected. Brown was disappointed but not thwarted.

On the Sunday morning (the 16th), the Old Man, as Anderson referred to Brown in his narrative, called the men to breakfast early, but as usual, he said a prayer and gave a sermon, like he did every other morning when he was at the farm. Also, like every other morning, he took roll call, read selections from the bible, and reconfirmed why the men were there. They were there because they heeded the call from God, he told them regularly. By virtue, we are all called upon, Brown admitted, but only few hear and even fewer act to conquer sin and evil.

Cowardice was the culprit at the core of inactivity. Brown went to Revelation 21:8 and read to the men: "But as for the cowardly, the faithless, the detestable, as for murderers, the sexually immoral, sorcerers, idolaters, and all liars, their portion will be in the lake that burns with fire and sulfur, which is the second death." It was their "duty as their brethren" to liberate the slaves. The Old Man typically spoke with a fiery passion, but today there was a momentousness that mounted in the service and struck a chord the rest of the day with the men. He left the men with one last thought that morning, "As it is said in Matthew 5:11-12, as if this is speaking directly to you, 'Blessed are you when others revile you and persecute you and utter all kinds of evil against you falsely on my account. Rejoice and be glad, for your reward is great in heaven, for so they persecuted the prophets who were before you.'" He looked up from his bible. "Gentlemen," he said, "mortal men may judge you, as they have always done those who came before them, but know that the only one whose judgment matters will see you as virtuous and pure of heart. Do not fear what awaits us. Fear is ungodly."

The men ate breakfast, and the girls began cleaning up the dishes, making trips around the table and in and out of the meeting room. They eventually disappeared for good, and the captain began giving orders and the general itinerary. He sent one man outside the door on the porch to keep watch and warn them if anyone approached. The rest of the men were alerted that there would be a council meeting later in the morning.

After the dismissal from breakfast and before the 10 o'clock meeting, the men went back into the attic and began packing their belongings together and becoming mentally prepared for the attack. At the meeting, Brown was curt in addressing the men, and then he turned the meeting over to Kagi, who conducted the formalities. Each had their role. After the meeting, Brown read the provisional constitution and had the men that he had never worked with before repeat an oath and swear allegiance. Men, like Hazlett, were given military duty and given a rank and a commission. As Hazlett had proven his loyalty and fearlessness, he was anointed as a lieutenant.

Kagi looked over the commissions as he gave them out, and if something was missing or if one was too new to the team to have it completed, he quickly scratched out the name and rank of one who did not report to duty and rewrote the name with the "required obligations."[1] Six captains were named—Stevens, Cook, Tidd, and the three Browns: Oliver, Owen, and Watson. Two lieutenants were named—Hazlett and Leeman—and the rest were private soldiers.

Some historians over the years have made mention that Brown chose only white men to be ranking members, yet if we are to take what Anderson said about Brown, picking only white men to be leaders was more a matter of qualifications of the candidates and sheer coincidence. Of Brown's dealings with his men, Anderson wrote:

> There was no milk-and-water sentimentality-no offensive contempt for the Negro—while working in his cause ... In John Brown's house, and in John Brown's presence, men from widely different parts of the continent met and united as one company, wherein no hateful prejudice dared intrude its ugly self. No ghost of a distinction found space to enter.[2]

They assembled to eat lunch around 11 o'clock, and once finished, Brown laid out the elaborate plan in full detail. His son Owen, F. J. Merriam, and Barclay Coppoc were to stay and guard the farmhouse. They were to wait for others to later return and take arms and supplies to the schoolhouse. Charles Tidd and John Cook were to cut communication to the town by tearing down the telegraph wires on the Maryland side first and then the Virginia side after the town was captured and secured. John Kagi and Aaron D. Stevens were to take the watchman of the bridge prisoner. Watson Brown and Stewart Taylor were to take position on the Potomac Bridge, and Oliver Brown and William Thompson were to do the same on the Shenandoah Bridge. Jeremiah Anderson and Dauphin Thompson were to take the Engine House until the rifle factory was secured. Hazlett and Edwin Coppoc were assigned the Armory, while Kagi and Copeland had the rifle factory through the night and await orders in the morning. Stevens and Anderson were then to proceed to arm slaves and take prisoners once the town was in the process of being locked down.

It was to be a coordinated effort that required stealth, silent communication, and a guerrilla-style sneak attack. Tactically, the plan needed to be pulled off quickly. No one spoke at dinner. There was deep concentration and focus.

"And, now gentlemen," he said, "let me impress this one thing upon your minds. You all know how dear life is to you, and how dear your life is to your friends. And in remembering that, consider that the lives of others are as dear to them as yours are to you. Do not, therefore, take the life of anyone, if you can possibly avoid it; but if it is necessary to take life in order to save your own, then make short work of it."[3]

At 8 p.m., under the cover of night, Brown gathered the men together one last time at Kennedy Farm and said, "Men, get on your arms; we will proceed to the Ferry."[4] He boarded a wagon, which would be used to load up the seized weapons. Pikes, a sledgehammer, and a crowbar were put in the wagon. He put on his old Kansas hat and said, "Come on, boys!"[5] The men filed in behind the wagon, two-by-two.

The plan called for many, but there was only a small, determined band. They marched through the brisk winds that were bringing a cold dampness. It swirled around them, hitting them from behind and then maneuvered to come head on into their faces. The day was in the high sixties, low seventies, but it started to get chilly when the sun went down with the rains blowing in. By the time they approached town after their 5-mile march, the temperature had dropped twenty-five or more degrees.

The winds brought a heavy and steady downpour. Adrenaline, focus, and the 105-minute walk kept them from realizing it when they stood high on a bluff overlooking the town. Instead of a nuisance, the men saw the storm as a blessing, for the slapping rains muffled and made more noise than they would make. As they always did before splitting off in other raids, they acknowledged one another; some shook hands, embraced to clap each other on the back, and then divided to go their separate ways and achieve the established tasks and maneuvers.

They cut the wires and then went to work. A deployment took the federal armory and arsenal. Hazlett and six others were left in charge of keeping guard of the arsenal while the other strategic milestones were to be achieved. Another group dispatched to round up hostages and free slaves. Others took to other parts of town, like Hall's Rifle Works and the railroad tracks coming into town. When it was all said and done, there were about sixty hostages, including George Washington's great-grandnephew, Lewis Washington. A small band of slaves were armed with pikes. The team was shorthanded, but so far, things were falling into place.

Ironically enough, however, a free black man was the first casualty. There are varying stories as to how Heyward Shepherd, a baggage handler from Winchester, Virginia, was shot and killed, but the end result was the same.

The time was between midnight and 1.30 a.m. when the Baltimore and Ohio train was pulling into town. Brown's men boarded the train and overtook it. Some assert that the train was stopped by Cook's hostage, the night watchman on the bridge, who broke free and flagged down the train. Either way, when Shepard went to investigate why the train was stopped, Brown's men held him up. It is said that he broke free and began running, and when they called for him to halt, he did not stop. They began shooting and mortally wounded him. They dragged him back to the train where he bled out and died around noon the next day.

Later, his refusal to take up arms and join in the fight to free slaves was celebrated by the United Daughters of the Confederacy with a monument erected in his honor in 1931, citing his "character and faithfulness." Considering the fact that Shepherd was not a faithful slave but a free black man, the motives of the organization are controversial and still under scrutiny today. The monument still stands across from the original John Brown fort on Potomac Street on the backside of the Wetland Museum in town. Some detest the memorial and protest it, calling it a tribute to slavery.

The raiders held the train up, deciding what should be done with it in their control. Finally, Brown sent word back to the men to allow the train to move on to its destination. Soon, it was back in D.C. reporting what had taken place in Harpers Ferry, and that was when an army commanded by Robert E. Lee was sent to reinstate order.

Before Lee's men arrived, the townspeople took matters into their own hands. Chaos ensued. Hazlett and Edwin Coppoc were able to take the Arsenal as planned, and a fight for it occurred where Hazlett ended up killing George Turner. As Hazlett approached, Turner was in the act of raising his rifle when Hazlett shot him. Coppoc escaped harm and joined Brown, who realized that the plan was failing. Brown, Coppoc, and others quickly rounded up nine prisoners and took shelter in the Engine House that is today referred to as "John Brown's Fort." Hazlett hid that afternoon in the thick underbrush and bushes behind the arsenal, like a mouse in weeds, until the scene quieted.

Hazlett heard townspeople raising hell in the streets. He felt the residents' sense of panic, drunken blood-lust, and unabated adrenaline. When he heard the commotion going on at the Engine House, he dared not make a move until the coast was clear. It seemed obvious that Brown and his men were either killed or captured. He laid low for a few hours. That night, he crept into the mountains that make up the landscape of the town. Early that next morning before the sun came up, he snuck back into the Arsenal building that overlooked the Engine House he knew Brown to be occupying, and there served as a sentinel sharpshooter with proper position. He held his position alone, dropping any real threat.

When the morning sun was fully risen, it became clearer as to what was happening. Men, women, and children could be seen leaving their homes in every direction, some seeking refuge among residents, and in quarters further away, others climbing up the hillsides and hurrying off in various directions, evidently impelled by a sudden fear, which was plainly visible in their countenances or in their movements.[6]

News spread quickly that the town was under siege and the name of one of the most infamous of raiders, John Brown, passed from person to person. As they were referred to, the band of Yankees was, as forecast by Frederick Douglass, geographically trapped in a snare, and they were already being made an example of what could happen when the institution of slavery was threatened. Word also spread that the Marines were on their way. This irritated some because they wanted to handle the brash insurrection how they saw fit without any type of government interference.

Throughout the day on the 17th, there were the spontaneous hostile encounters that could be heard and the various sniper pop shots dropping targets, scattering victims randomly around the town and down by the Engine House. Much to Hazlett's chagrin, Osborne found his way back to the Arsenal, and the two hid out there to see how things would transpire.

Tense hours compounded and stretched into a day, and it was around noon on the 18th when Lee and his force approached the Engine House and ran ladders up to the roof for position. Hazlett and Osborne watched the entire event unfold. It was apparent that they were going to take the Armory back, take Brown at the Engine House, quell the insurrection, and restore order in the town.

"What do we do, sir?" Osborne asked Hazlett, deferring to his rank.

"We wait," Hazlett said.

"For what, sir? This mission has failed. We are being overtaken. It appears time to admit defeat, retreat back to Kennedy Farm, and regroup with the others."

"We wait for Captain Brown's orders," Hazlett gritted.

"Sir, our men are dead. We are all that remain. If John Brown is still alive over there, there is no doubt that he would be unable to relate any order to any of us, let alone enforce it, if, indeed, any of us are still alive to carry out an order."

"Then we wait for word from the next in line, that'll be Captain Kagi," Hazlett insisted.

"Before Captain Brown was made prisoner, Captain Kagi ceased to live."[7]

"How do you know that?"

"You heard the firefight at the bridge, and he never made it to the rifle factory. Even if he is still alive, all our communication between our post and him had been long cut off. We could not aid Captain Brown by remaining."[8]

Hazlett thought a bit, thinking about how far they had come and what was at stake. They were right on the precipice of a coup so enormously threatening that Robert E. Lee had to be sent to stop them. Now that the Engine House was totally closed off and without being sure of how badly wounded Captain Brown was but sure he was either dead or in the hands of the government, it was safe to say that the mission had failed and that retreat was imminent. However, that last shred of doubt kept Hazlett at the scene.

"We might be able to aid him by going back to Kennedy Farm, devise a plan for his succor, or our experience might become available on some future occasion. There is but little two of us can do against so many, and that our turn to be taken must come," pleaded Osborne.[9]

Hazlett thought it all over again and finally turned to nod. There was a brief consideration of what they were leaving behind—thousands of dollars' worth of weapons and the responsibility of restoring liberty and freedom—but they gathered themselves to get ready for an escape back to the farm. They only took the arms and rounds that they came with, minus those Hazlett spent during the brief standoff and sniper post that felt like an eternity. The two headed out the back door, looking both ways through squinting eyes that hurt from the brightness of the day. They climbed the wall and ran to the train tracks. They stayed sandwiched between the tracks and the Shenandoah range to keep their northern bearing. Along the way, they counted what ammunition they had left. They had a little over twenty rounds between the two of them.

There can be up to a 40-degree swing in temperatures in the region. During the day, it can get into the high-to-mid-70s, but at night, it could plummet down close to freezing, blanketing everything with a heavy frost by morning. As the sun was setting, the temperature was beginning to drop.

Even though it is early autumn, the underbrush of the woods had dried and hardened by the long drought of August. Jagger bushes reached across to the tracks and mercilessly tore at Albert's arms and legs as he tried to pass. Mostly, he could just rip himself away, leaving what looked and burned like cat scratches wherever it could grab at the skin. At times, he had to stop to pick and pull himself free from their stubborn hold.

Urgently, Osborne grabbed Hazlett by the arm and the two stopped dead in their tracks. Just ahead, a man was crossing, his rifle down at his side. The two ambushed him with their weapons drawn. The man gasped, dropped his weapon, and put his hands up as if to say, "Don't shoot."

Without a word, Hazlett picked up the dropped gun as Osborne grabbed the man and searched for a sidearm. There was none. "You just came from the Ferry, did you not?" Osborne gruffly said.

"I did," the man responded.

"Is it over? What happened at the rifle factory?" Osborne asked, thinking that that was the true last bastion.

"Yes, the fighting is over. One of your men tried to run as the militia tried to retake the factory, but he was shot and killed while trying to flee across the Shenandoah River."

Osborne looked at Albert, "Kagi," he said. They both knew what that meant. They had made the right decision by leaving when they did. They would assuredly have been captured or killed at the scene.

"All said and done," the man continued, "at least seventy people were killed these past three days, perhaps more, with many more wounded and maimed by the encounter."

It is of note that there has never been a confirmed count of the dead. Some died from wounds and infection days if not weeks later. Some newspaper accounts downplayed the death total, and the reports ranged from five to twenty being killed. Anderson and Hazlett said that at least fifty were killed, accounting for the amount each man was armed and the amount of gunshot volleys that ensued throughout the course of the event.

"The order of the town had been restored by Lee's men," the man said almost in defiance. "The crazy, bearded man held up in the Engine House had been captured. One of his sons is dead. The other was wounded when he emerged from the engine house. It was said that when he fell, he had a white flag of surrender in his hand. It was just as well that he died right there in the Engine House, too, because he was a dead man anyway."

Hazlett Portrait: This is the only known picture of Absalom Hazlett (September 21, 1837–March 16, 1860). (*Library of Congress*)

Historical Marker Dedication: Photographer Harry Hunt attended the ceremony and documented the event on Flickr. This was the cover of the program that had information on those responsible for the marker, with a short biography of Hazlett and the itinerary inside. (*Courtesy Harry Hunt*)

John Brown Mural: The classic painting *Tragic Prelude* by John Steuart Curry was a large mural painted for the rotunda of the Kansas State Capitol. Rich in color and symbolism, Curry's work (which is in the public domain) is still a popular item on t-shirts, posters, and hundreds of websites. (*Library of Congress*)

Opposite: Hazlett Ceremony: Harry Hunt wrote, "Posing with the newly unveiled historical marker are (left to right) Ken Truitt; Ms. Denise Jennings-Doyle (Blairsville Passport to Freedom Underground Railroad Experience); Seth Gibson; Ms. Karen James (Coordinator of African American History Program, Pennsylvania Historical and Museum Commission); Ms. Chris Catalfamo (Board of Directors, Historical and Genealogical Society of Indiana County); Marna Conrad." (*Courtesy Harry Hunt*)

ABSALOM (ALBERT) HAZLETT
(1837-1860)
A staunch abolitionist, Hazlett became a lieutenant in John Brown's provisional army and participated in the raid on Harper's Ferry Arsenal in 1859. He was captured, tried, convicted, and hanged for his involvement following the failed Harper's Ferry attack. This incident, intended to arm slaves to fight for their own freedom, was a major catalyst for the outbreak of the Civil War. Hazlett was born and raised near here.
PENNSYLVANIA HISTORICAL AND MUSEUM COMMISSION 2009

Grave: L. A. Brandebury stands with Lewis Foreman and his father, James, who witnessed the mass burial and led the party to the gravesite along the bank of the Shenandoah. (*Courtesy Saranac Lake Welcome Center*)

Funeral: Rev. Joshua Young, D.D. (hat off, bald with long white beard), gives the benediction. (*Library of Congress*)

Trunk: The contents of the bodies were packed in cotton and excelsior in this trunk and shipped to Lake Placid, N.Y. (*Courtesy Saranac Lake Welcome Center*)

Here is a rude plan of the building and its yard :

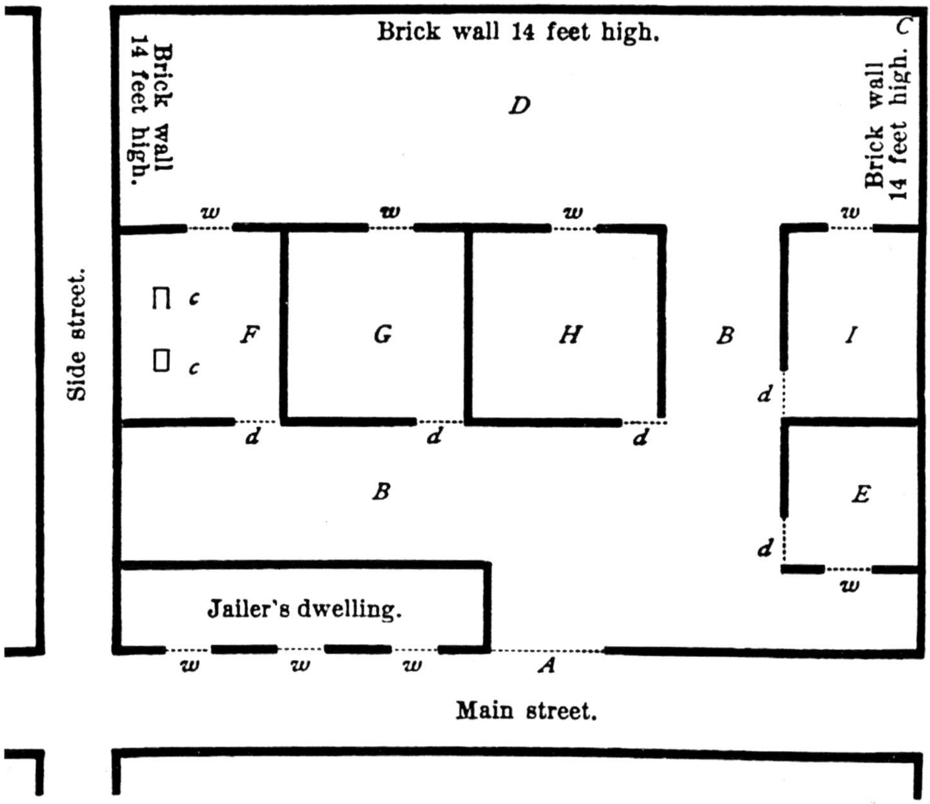

A Main entrance; *B* Space between walls, Avis's house, and the jail building; *C* Point of wall which Cook and Coppoc reached on the night of Dec. 15th in their attempt to escape; *D* Jail yard *d d d d d*, cell doors; *E* Reception-room; *F* Cell occupied by Brown and Stevens, afterwards by the latter and Hazlett; *G* Cell of Green and Copeland; *H* Cell of Coppoc and Cook; *I* Cell first occupied by Albert Hazlett, *w w w*, *w w*, windows, those of cells look into the jail yard; *c c* cots of Brown and Stevens.

Rude Plan: Richard Hinton wrote an authoritative work, *John Brown and His Men,* and it was published on December 31, 1894. This illustration comes from page 342 of that book.

Courthouse and Jail: Again from *Frank Leslie's Illustrated Newspaper*, there is a picture of the prison, the guardhouse, and the courthouse in Charlestown, W.V. The caption reads, "The Prison is on the extreme left." (*Library of Congress*)

Hanging: *Frank Leslie's Illustrated Newspaper* ran the story on the hanging of Stevens and Hazlett. (*West Virginia State Archives*)

Harpers Ferry: The National Parks Service photo shows John Brown's Fort to the left in the photo. It can no longer be considered "fully authentic" because it was dismantled, moved, and reassembled several times. Also, no photo can give the full scope of the highs and lows of the terrain. The raiders would have entered from the extreme right of the photo from Maryland, along the Potomac, and then across the bridge. (*N.P.S.*)

Portrait of Osborne Anderson. (*Library of Congress*)

Ritner House: The Ritner family are noted Underground Railroad activists. Mary Ritner, widowed after the death of Abram, ran the boarding house as early as 1852. It was during one of his stays in Chambersburg that Brown tried to recruit Douglass. (*Courtesy Ann Hull, Director of the Franklin County Historical Society*)

Gun: The Colt revolver that was bartered for a night's sleep. (*The Kansas Historical Society*)

Overlooking the Town of Harpers Ferry: This photo from the National Parks Service is used on the Tripadvisor website for promotional purposes. On the left is the Shenandoah River that meets and becomes the Potomac River at the point. The arsenal was along the Potomac. (*N.P.S.*)

Brown's Fort: The original Engine House faced the Armory along the Potomac. *John Brown's Fort* was painted to encourage tourism. It was later reassembled and reconstructed where it sits today. (*Library of Congress*)

Attic: Along with the pikes that were stored at headquarters, there were plenty of Sharps rifles, one of which can be seen hanging along the back wall. (*Courtesy Sprigg Lynn and Dawn Gardner*)

Opposite above: The Kennedy Farm sits in Washington County, Maryland. It was restored and made available for tours by South Lynn and his son, South, Jr., and Sprigg. (*Courtesy Sprigg Lynn and Dawn Gardner*)

Opposite below: S. Green: The mannequin of Shields Green sits on his cot in the attic of the Kennedy Farmhouse. (*Courtesy Sprigg Lynn and Dawn Gardner*)

Sharps Rifle and Pike: Picture from *Frank Leslie's Illustrated Newspaper* depicting a Sharps rifle, a pike, and the little schoolhouse. (Library of Congress)

Tour: Sprigg Singleton Lynn giving a tour of the attic. He is holding a pike that Brown intended to issue to slaves because the pikes did not require training for use. (*Courtesy Sprigg Lynn and Dawn Gardner*)

James Montgomery portrait. (*Library of Congress*)

When it came time to leave the tracks to cross the mountains, they ran through any stream they could find, assuring themselves that they were going the right way by trudging against the current. They were thirsty and exhausted. There were times they had to secure their prisoner and basically drag him to his feet to push on because he was so desperately tired and worn. He had a long day of fighting and was scarred by his first experience with human blood and death, and now he was on the run like a fugitive without a chance to process what he had been through.

They moved as quickly as they could to try to reach the mountains and gain the advantage of position. They knew they could rest once covered by the rocks and nightfall. The hostage surveyed the mountains and estimated his chances. He sensed that this was the end for him because they had made the safety of the mountains. The realization overcame him. "Please don't kill me," he blurted out.

"We're not thoughtless murderers, you louse!" said Hazlett in anger.

"Then," he paused, "I won't make the mountains," he pleaded.

"What do you mean?" pressed Anderson.

"I will never make it over the mountains. I won't be of any help to you anyway. I feared that you were going to kill me, but if you are not, please, I beg of you, please let me go. In the name of liberty. Please, it has been a terrible few days for me. Just turn me loose. Of course, keep the rifle. Just let me go home, please."

The two considered. A hostage at this point would be useless to their cause, and even up to this point, the man has been nothing more than a burden than a help. "Look here," said Hazlett, "we will turn you loose, but you get home and keep your mouth shut about us. You never saw us, ya hear?"

"Of course not, gentlemen, not a word of our encounter," he responded. "I see you are believers in liberty. Bless your souls."

Hazlett glared at him and gave him a shove. The man disappeared into the underbrush, giving one last look before ducking out of sight. Hazlett turned to Osborne to continue heading into the mountains. As they began their zigzag climb up the mountainside in search of a lookout and resting place, they looked over their shoulders and saw the man in the flat, heading back the way they had come, back toward the railroad tracks. As they stopped and waited to watch him, they sensed the man was acting more like he had just escaped instead of being let go. He gave a glance back, saw the two men watching him, and began to run into the woods and the stream that had brought them out into a little clearing.

Scratching and clawing their way through mountainous terrain, they made it to the point to where the rocks began to jut more steeply, and they could get a sweeping view of the clearing between the foothills and the woods. It was there that they made their resting place for the night.

Albert took off his boots and socks heavy with wetness. They estimated that they had about twenty minutes to half an hour of daylight, so any search party would also be looking to get where they were going by sundown.

No sooner had they talked about the prospects of a search party when they heard the clamor coming out of the woods and into the clearing. The men stopped at the woods, careful not to be sitting ducks. They were confused, and some pointed one way, while others pulled and pointed toward the other.

Hazlett and Anderson had practiced for this moment; with their position, they could plunk them off one by one. Hazlett lined up one and squeezed the trigger. With efficiency of rounds in mind, these shots were not meant to warn but to kill. Their gut instincts and suspicions when releasing their hostage were correct. He went into the town and told the authorities, and now they were here to engage.

Hazlett's first victim was down, so another had attended to assess his condition. That man was shot. Another ran to him. Osborne sighted the attendee and fired. The man never flinched but just dropped dead. No one ran to his aid as the first man was being dragged back to the safety of the woods' edge. The mass confusion told the two snipers that the small posse had no idea from whence the shots rang.

After some time, it appeared that the company had reorganized and orchestrated an attack on the hillside. They had fanned out and were approaching the mountain. The two fired at will. It is best to read Anderson's own words:

> We poured ... some well-directed shots. It was not so dark but that we could see one bite the dust now and then when others would run to aid them instantly, particularly the wounded. Some lay where they fell, undisturbed, which satisfied us that they were dead. The troops returned our fire, but it was random shooting, as we were concealed from their sight by the rocks and bushes. Interchanging of shots continued for some minutes, with much spirit, when it became dark, and they went down into the town. After their return to the Ferry, we could hear the drum beating for a long time; an indication of their triumph, we supposed. Hazlett and I remained in our position three hours, before we dared venture down.[10]

It was dark and the rains coming in made the night that much darker; navigating down the mountainous terrain of the outcrops in Harpers Ferry was treacherous business. They snuck through the back part of town, down further to the bottom of the hill to the railroad tracks. Then they doubled-back, crossed over though town, and passed the sawmill to the Virginia side of the Potomac. There in the water, they found a boat and paddled over the river to Maryland.

Heading north on the run, they laid low during the day, carefully creeping their way along parts of the Underground Railroad and hoping to stumble upon a host to put them up for the night. Yet so far, they had not been that lucky. Instead, they basically ran all night to get ahead of the authorities, if that was even possible. The authorities lay ahead, behind, all over—that is how the institution worked. They felt like there was no escape. Their only hope was that more raiders were on the run and the authorities would be as confused as a bird hunter startled by inadvertently flushing fluttering doves, unable to focus on any particular one.

Under an oppressively gray sky, they knew that more rain was imminent. They were soaked from the inside out from sweat, so the rain would soak them from the outside in, making sure that they would chafe and be even more uncomfortable on the run.

Moving quickly through the night, Albert's socks and boots never got a chance to fully dry out. He would take his boots and socks off in brief periods when they would stop to rest in thicker cover, but they never really had enough time to completely dry. He winced from the dampness of the dressings as he put them back on to get on the move. With the cold wetness of the rain, drying out would only be possible if they found an overnight refuge by a conductor on the railroad.

Hazlett could feel an uncomfortable rub that eventually worked up blisters on the knuckles of his toes, his Achilles heel, and the sides of his big toe joint, but the skin did not work free, so though they nagged, he could not put them out of mind to forge ahead. They felt like minor burns. What bothered him more than the blisters were the brambles and thorny briers that surrounded large fields and seemed to jump at him, catch hold, and bite through his red shirt and grey trousers. He quickly grew tired of picking burrs from his shirt.

The trouble with the fields, however, was the danger of plain sight. The clearer lowlands made for much easier travel but staying higher on the foothills was the safest mode of travel. The main roads and pathways were obviously easier travel, so the two used as many roads, paths, and tracks as they could for expediency.

The sun was going down and there was still a nagging chill in the air. They thought that now was a good time to rest for a few hours before pushing further in the night. Hazlett tried to rest his mind, but he could not clear his thoughts. He settled for just resting his tired body.

They figured that of the twenty-one men who took part in the raid, few were alive, free, and on the run like they were. All along, they assumed death to be their sentence. Their burning passion to awaken the resistance and rely on the promise of freedom put them on a collision course with an institution that had the resources to crush them into oblivion. He did not think that any of them underestimated the power of the institution of slavery, but fundamentally, they had. Running for their lives illuminated the fear that slaves endured, the hopelessness that either broke them or enraged them forward.

Hazlett also knew that institutional power to be an unreliable entity because behind it, there is a human foil—empathy. Humans build institutions to hide or reinforce their fears and emotions, but buried within every federation, there is a softer side where fear breeds empathetic opposition. To the empathetic abolitionist, their country had failed them through the corruption of greed, morals, and hubris manifesting itself in the form of slavery. They viewed their country as a callous society void of empathy for human beings broken in spirit to endure what slaves had to endure. The south constructed and coldly legislated the institution to legitimize their perversion of scruples; therefore, slavery never showed it could be ashamed of its cruelty. Slavery hid behind a law and justified itself through a self-ordained superiority. Slavery gave no indication of mercy or the willingness or ability change, nor did it have to.

That is why Hazlett saw that slavery needed to be defeated. It had no face. It relied on objectivity, thus it needed to be met and defeated with objectivity. Empathy for the slave had to conquer the institution. He had joined a force with John Brown that sealed his fate long before he tried to calm his mind and rest in the woods while being on the run. As he rested, a shiver periodically ran up his spine, either from the penetrating, wet cold or from something deeper down.

The Fall from Grace Contrast of John E. Cook (October 20–25, 1859)

As Hazlett chose his fate long before being caught, he chose a scheme that would keep him from ratting out his friends. The ingenious simplicity of denying identity, even when proven flimsy, made any type of confession of guilt impossible, thus making it impossible to implicate his friends. This was how Hazlett emboldened the cause—fight with courage and sneaky intelligence. That would be his one, last contribution to the fight, knowing it was a fight to the death.

Yet not all of them gave the same fight, forgetting regality and standing for a cause. Regardless of how noble their ideals and how piously John Brown used to talk about doing God's work, it seemed less than stoic when Hazlett got word from other abolitionists in jail that John E. Cook was a turncoat, giving names and the inner workings of the plan once he was caught.

John E. Cook was a law clerk by trade. He was known to be a womanizer in his hometown, but he carried respect among the raiders for being an excellent marksman. Brown trusted him to be the eyes and ears of the group and sent him as a plant in the town of Chambersburg and later Harpers Ferry to gather information and pass it back to Kennedy Farm, where the men were hunkered down.

When the plan fell apart and it became every man for himself, it was painfully obvious to Cook that unlike the others on the run, the townspeople knew him and could easily identify him, especially his prominent captive, Lewis Washington. Cook took Washington hostage and because he was related to the first president and Cook had stolen his prized pistol once owned by LaFayette, revenge seemed inevitable. So, when Washington was rescued by J. E. B. Stuart's unit at Harpers Ferry, Cook's name was one of the first mentioned.

The next morning, Washington swore in an affidavit that Cook was directly responsible for his kidnapping and robbery. He also wrote that "Cook is now a fugitive from justice and is fleeing and attempting to escape in the state of Maryland, Pennsylvania, or New York."[11] Newspaper reports and handbills were circulated throughout the three states offering a $1,000 reward, sponsored by Virginia Governor Henry Wise for Cook's arrest.

The description in the newspaper read, "Five feet four to six inches high; weighs 132 pounds; walks with his breast projecting forward, and his head leaning toward the right side; has light hair, with a small growth around the upper lip, is of sallow complexion, and has a sharp, narrow face."[12] He was identified in the papers as Brown's chief aid.

In a speech in Richmond, Wise in full detail accurately described Cook's spying mission, his census of slaves, and his surveillance of the armory; he even accused him of murdering a slave "who attempted to escape from him."[13] It was realized early by authorities that those who were not killed were on the run, so it was assumed that there were more unidentifiable men scattered about.

While on the run with fellow raiders Charles Tidd, Francis Merrimam, Barclay Coppoc, and Owen Brown, Cook aggravated his cohorts with his incessant jabber, Tidd especially. He had blue eyes and blond curly hair that made him look younger than he really was, and though he commanded respect, he got very little from the small band. Even though Brown ranked Cook highly, Tidd refused to respect him. Due to his law school education in Brooklyn, his New York arrogance, his general cockiness, his know-it-all attitude, and his expectation that others would go along with anything he said, Cook became agitated that the group refused to make more time staying on the roads rather than picking their way through the dense underbrush of the woods. The others believed his days in law school and pampered, upper-class upbringing did not prepare him for these experiences, so they overrode his suggestions. He begrudgingly conceded and played it safe by slowly working through the brush, as his colleagues proposed.

Like Hazlett and Osborne, who the group speculated to be on the run, they rested and hid low in the thickets or high in the mountain tops during the days, and they trudged on in the cover of the graying of dusk or the blackness of night. Yet unlike Hazlett and Osborne, they avoided traveled passages.

Like the slaves who allowed the stars to be their guides, so Tidd, Cook, Merriam, Coppoc, and Owen Brown crept their way cautiously to the north to Cook's choice destination—Chambersburg, Pennsylvania, a known station on the Underground Railroad. Also, Cook's wife and child were there, so though going westward toward Ohio made more sense to everyone else, they sympathized with him and followed along with that one suggestion.

Merriam and Coppoc were inherent followers. Merriam had only one good eye, losing the other as a child. Brown knew him to be too frail, "erratic and unbalanced" to be trusted for combat.[14] In fact, when Merriam with his syphilis-scarred face first approached Brown to join ranks, Brown denied him. It was not until later, when Brown was desperate for cash, that he accepted Merriam in with a healthy donation to the cause provided by Merriam's rich parents. While in flight, he was a constant drag on the group because he regularly needed help crossing quick-moving streams or scaling rugged mountain terrain.

Barclay Coppoc was the brother of Edwin. They were Iowa Quakers, and though Edwin was strong and capable, his brother suffered from "consumption." Brown took both in but limited Barclay's involvement because of how winded he would get doing menial tasks. He never complained, though, and throughout this journey, he kept pace and compensated for his lack of ability.

At last, Coppoc and Merriam, despite their willingness to follow, put their foot down as to how they would travel once Cook demanded that they travel by road. An argument began heating up, and Tidd intervened and took over the fight. It got so heated between Cook and Tidd that Owen had to get between them to keep it from coming to blows. Owen sensed that at this point the group was about to totally disband and go their separate ways. "It was not easy work to separate Cook and Tidd," Brown later recalled, but he succeeded in persuading them to wait "to have it out [until] they could do it without endangering others."[15]

As history documents and confirms, Tidd was right. Authorities and bounty hunters dispersed to capture the fugitives, took the easy way, and stuck to the roads for traveling and canvassing. With Chambersburg's reputation for being the obvious destination, it was one of the first places handbills were posted and bounty hunters flocked, so the race was on to get to Chambersburg. For bounty hunters, roads and railroad tracks were the answer.

Owen was the only raider in the group who had once before made the trek from Maryland to Chambersburg, but maybe because of his fragility and deformed arm, they gravitated to listening to Cook, who took them extra days out of their way to make them almost a full week on the run. Provisions were low. The dry biscuits and sugar that the Brown girls had packed for them were gone days ago, and they resorted to looting fields and orchards and eating whatever forgotten fruits and vegetables were left in the fields to rot. They even raided a henhouse or two, and then they climbed high into the Cumberland Valley Mountains to build a small fire and cook them.

Cook was injured after falling down the steep hillside crossing into Pennsylvania. He limped along behind the others. They hiked for over 100 miles and were about 15 miles outside of Chambersburg when Owen suggested a plan. He and Tidd, who was perhaps the ablest of the crew, convinced Cook with his injuries, Merriam with his frailties, and Coppoc with his consumption to lay low and wait for them to go on and scout out the best entry point into town.

As Tidd and Brown were advancing, they smelled doughnuts cooking from a farmhouse they were passing. Tidd was overcome with hunger and exhaustion and because of the "lard-laden air" he "vowed he wouldn't go a step farther without food," but Brown convinced him otherwise.[16] Brown had no confidence that Tidd could bluff his way out of a sticky situation, but he knew who could.

They went back to the small *ad hoc* camp and approached Cook because "he could wield the glibbest tongue and tell the best story," according to Brown.[17] Cook went back to the farmhouse and made fast friends during what he later called a "splendid visit." The men worried as he spent several hours with the generous hosts, but he returned with "a couple of loaves of bread ... some good boiled beef, and a pie" that he purchased from the inhabitants of the farmhouse.

Full of himself and giddy after the first real meal that any of them had eaten in over a week, Cook brandished the "old-fashioned, one-barrel" pistol that he stole from Washington.[18] He laughed and joked about how

Washington did not want to give up the pistol because it once belonged to Revolutionary War hero General Marquis de Lafayette. Cook gloated about how he withheld the pistol from Old Man Brown, and as if in celebration, he randomly fired a shot in the air.

"What the hell are you doing, you fool!" Tidd yelled. "The people at the farmhouse will easily hear gunshots. Nothing good can come of this. Don't shoot that thing again!"

Cook took it as a challenge to his ego. "I know what I am doing," he said and cracked off another shot with his own Colt revolver. "I'm not taking orders from any of you, especially you." He popped off another round.

Tidd got up and got into Cook's face. Merriam went to stop the encounter but was somehow thrown aside and onto the ground. Trying to diffuse the situation before it ended in a fistfight or a gunfight, Owen and Barclay rushed between them.

Throughout the course of the following day, the two bickered and picked at one another. Now that they were getting close to Chambersburg, Cook lamented seeing his family again, but everyone knew that the boarding house would be a *bona fide* trap. They convinced Cook that it would be smart to be cautious and take the entrance into town slowly.

At mid-afternoon, the group stopped at a stream, and Coppoc volunteered to strike out and get provisions for them. Brown intervened, convincing the group once again that Cook was best suited for the job, and because he wanted to get away from Tidd, Cook eagerly jumped at the opportunity. Brown gave him several dollars, then Cook took a revolver and headed out about "three or four o'clock in the afternoon," as Brown remembered.[19]

Initially, they thought nothing of it when he did not return within hours, since the episode at the farmhouse took hours, but now they began to worry as the day gave way to dusk. They waited "till nine o'clock, till midnight, and still he did not come," Owen Brown wrote. They thought that he may have gotten lost, so they "lingered about, calling and watching for him till at least two o'clock in the morning."[20]

Fearing the unexpected, they dismantled any plans along with their camp and began packing up and taking what they could carry with careful consideration, given Merriam and Coppoc's limited capabilities. Yet, assuredly, Tidd made sure he got Lafayette's single-shot pistol. Coincidentally, they met up with Osborne Anderson, who was traveling alone since leaving Hazlett, and all of them ultimately made it to safety in the north.

Charles Plummer Tidd, though he was unconvinced of the viability of the plan to attack Harpers Ferry, took part in the raid. He followed his common sense, which was directed by his instincts. He made it into Pennsylvania and found his freedom. He was freely consulting in the plans for the rescue of Stevens and Hazlett during the time ideas were floating about to break them out of jail. Later in writing about the incident at Harpers Ferry, Mrs. Annie Brown Adams described Tidd: "He was by no means handsome. He had a quick temper but was kindhearted. His rages soon passed and then he tried all he could to repair damages. He was a fine singer and of strong family affections."[21]

Barclay Coppoc made up his mind that he was going to go back home to Springdale, Iowa, which he did. He left the group, went to Shippensburg, and from there hopped trains to Philadelphia and from there on to Iowa. About three months after he got home, a requisition was received by Iowa Governor Samuel Kikwood from the Virginia Governor's office requesting the return of Barclay Coppoc for his involvement in the Harpers Ferry raid. Kirkwood deemed the requisition devoid of legal form, and he refused action on it until properly formed. By the time the corrected papers returned, Coppoc was gone.

Later, he returned to Kansas, helped runaway Missouri slaves, and nearly lost his life in the process. He joined the Union army, and that is what sealed his fate. Shortly after on July 24, 1861, he was on the train that went into the Platte River. Confederates had burned supports to the trestle that spanned 40 feet. As the train approached, the trestle collapsed under the weight. Some accounts say that Coppoc died on the scene, some say he died weeks later from internal injuries, and some say that he was held captive as a Confederate prisoner until he died years after the war.

In March 1874, Owen Brown was the only living member of the party; Anderson died three years earlier in 1871. The *Atlantic Monthly* ran a story by Ralph Keeler, who visited the farms and interviewed Owen and his older brother John, Jr. It was the first time that he had ever spoken of the raid in twelve years. Even in his detailed account that ran some twenty-three pages, he did not incriminate anyone. He died of pneumonia on January 8, 1889, in Pasadena, California. He was sixty-four.

The same could not be said of "Judas," as some on the team called him. When Cook was caught, he attempted to save his own life with a detailed written confession. When Cook left Owen, Coppoc, Tidd, and Merriam in search of food to bring back to their hideout in the woods, he hiked several miles through rough terrain and thickets. He neared a clearing by the borough of Mont Aldo. If confronted, he already had his story ready. He was a hunter who had gotten lost and was looking for provisions.

In the clearing standing around talking was a group of ironworkers from the borough. Cook felt uneasy about approaching them, for he knew that he could not overtake a group to get away. However, he had already hiked a distance, been gone hours, and feared that he would return to camp empty-handed. Among the men in the clearing, though, was Daniel Logan.

Daniel Logan was an opportunist who paid attention to the handbills and had cashed in on runaway slaves and fugitives from the law as a result. He knew that some men from the raid at Harpers Ferry were on the run and had seen Cook's handbill, so the moment Cook emerged from the woods, he told his manager at the forge, Cleggett Fitzhugh, "That's Captain Cook; we must arrest him; the reward is $1,000."[22]

As Cook came closer, he addressed the group, "Hey, there, fellas," he said with his typical charm and bravado. "You don't happen to know where I could replenish my stock of bread and bacon, do you?"

Logan quickly stepped up and answered him, "Why, as a matter of fact, yes, we do. Lucky for you, I was just about to head back into town. If you want to come along, I will take you to the company store."

"Well," Cook hesitated, "if you just point me in that direction, I can make it alone."

"That might be so," said Logan, "but you will need to have a worker vouch for you before you're able to make a purchase. Like I said, it is my company's store."

Cook thought a bit more. "Well," he thought about turning around and leaving. "If that's the case," he started, realizing this was his last chance to turn and run. "Well, lead the way."

Logan smiled, reached out his hand, and grabbed Cook's to pull him closer to pat him on the back. He turned to Fitzhugh and pulled him by the arm and said, "This here's my manager, Fitzhugh. We were about to go into town together." The three of them began walking to town.

They reached the top of a hillside where Cook could look down and see a small town nestled in the knolls with a smokestack billowing black. Logan maneuvered himself behind Cook and snatched up his small frame. He latched onto him, while Cook later in his confession described the feeling as if being caught in a vice. He could not move or reach for his pistol.

While in Logan's grip, Fitzhugh began patting Cook down and disarming him. "Wait! Wait!" he hollered, struggling against the force of Logan. "What the hell are you guys doing?"

"You, my friend, are under arrest," Logan answered.

"Under arrest? Me?" he asked, "Why do you arrest me?"

"You don't think we know who you are? Why, you're Captain Cook. That's why we are arresting you." Stripped of his weapons, they took Cook to Fitzhugh's house and gave him a "cold meal."[23] Rifling through Cook's coat pockets, the two found some papers and receipts. One of the papers was a printed commission, marked No. 4, as a captain under Brown's "Provisional Government." That document read:

> HEADQUARTERS—WAR DEPARTMENT
> Near Harpers Ferry, Md Whereas: John E. Cook has been nominated a captain in the Armory established under the provisional government. Now, Therefore, in pursuance of the authority vested in us by said Constitution, we do hereby appoint and commission said John E. Cook, captain.
> Given at the office of the Secretary of War, this day, October 15th, 1959.
> John Brown, Commander in Chief
> H. Kagi, Secretary of War[24]

"Don't you know that creating a parallel government is a treasonous felony punishable by death, Mr. Cook?" Logan mocked. Looking through the other scraps of papers with some pulled from his pocketbook, they found two receipts. Both had Cook's signature on them—clear, legible, and in its bold uniqueness. "Eureka!" Logan celebrated. Already convinced that they had enough proof to retrieve the reward, Logan found a small piece of parchment with a string tied on one end. On it was a handwritten inscription that read:

> One of a pair of pistols presented by Gen. LaFayette to Gen. Washington, and worn by Gen. W. during the Revolution—descended to Judge Washington, and by him bequeathed to George C. Washington, and by him to Lewis W. Washington, 1854.[25]

Without the pistol and only knowing of the Colt they found on Cook's person, the document made no sense to Logan or Fitzhugh, but they assuredly would keep it and present it as evidence to the authorities once they were to reach Chambersburg.

They held Cook captive overnight and in the morning, they "bundled" him into Fitzhugh's open buggy and took him to Chambersburg.[26] Once there, the evidence was presented. Lewis Washington immediately recognized the parchment and could identify Cook as one of the men that took him hostage. Crushed under the weight of incriminating evidence and the threat of the gallows, Cook agreed to write a sixteen-page confession.

In his confession and in full detail, Cook outlined the plans for the insurrection and the roles that each man was to play. Given that information, it could be deduced all those who were able to escape and still be unaccounted for and so fugitives of the law. Cook hoped that the confession would save not only his hide but his soul, and he wrote it as such, identifying a hierarchy that would designate Brown as the sole leader and the others mere manipulated pawns in his scheme. It was a confession skillfully written to confess to nothing, while in the process throwing his cohorts under the proverbial bus.

8

Preening the Nest

Brown Attempts to Garner Support (July 1859)

John Brown had finally pulled his resources together. He raised money from the "Secret Six," who was financially backing the endeavor, and he put together a full-fledged plan fleshed out with a roster and specific details. He now was beginning to recruit able leaders and more men of action. So far, not many men reported for duty following the recruiting efforts of John Kagi and the letters he wrote to call the men to action. John Jr. was also out canvassing and drafting soldiers, and the Old Man saw the necessity to go out and personally gain support and, hopefully, manpower. He had to walk the fine line of getting the word out and jeopardizing the secrecy of the mission.

Since Augustus Wattles and James Montgomery had called on his services during the border wars in Sugar Mound, Kansas, and Linn County, Missouri, in the fall of 1858, Brown went to pitch them to engage their services for the surprise he had laying ahead for the country at Harpers Ferry.

Brown brought with him maps, plans, facts, and notes collected for analysis. Wattles and Montgomery were both interested in what the idea was that Brown had to share. Brown thought that Montgomery would be an easy sell. Guerilla warfare was Montgomery's specialty, and he had been known to take calculated risks. With Montgomery came a considerable number of henchmen, so if he could enlist the help of Montgomery, his chances of pulling off this coup improved greatly by sheer numbers and manpower alone.

The Wattles' abode made a good meeting point at Sugar Mound, and Wattles carried a certain amount of political clout and credibility. Wattles was an exceptional fundraiser and contributor to campaigns. Back in

1841, he raised enough money to buy 30,000 acres to create a colony of African Americans called Cartagena. To get Wattles on board meant a steady, reliable stream of cash.

"The armory sits down by the Potomac River," said Brown. "It could be an easy escape if we face trouble." As usual, Brown spoke passionately and eloquently, but Wattles and Montgomery just stared at him in utter disbelief. It was a grand, unorthodox scheme. They listened intently as Brown laid out the details of the plan, where the men would be stationed, the positions of the vital cargo of weapons and supplies, the methods of attack, and all other phases of the attack.

"I'm sorry, John," said Montgomery after Brown finished. "I can't take part in this, and I strongly urge that you not take part in this enterprise either." Wattles chimed in.

> I have to agree with James. I don't even see the prudence in funding this endeavor. This plan not only sounds like it relies heavily on coincidence, impeccable timing, and just dumb luck, it is a certain death warrant. There will be a level of violence required to pull this off that I am not inclined to agree to, as well. You say you can sneak in and out, but ultimately it will take brute force and violence to achieve this goal. I oppose initiating a plan that will take the carnage necessary to complete this if the timing of it doesn't go just right. You have known that I have always disagreed with your audacity to think that violence is a means to an end of slavery. Evil cannot be stopped with evil. Light conquers dark. We had this discussion in this very room before you wrote the *Parallels*.

Brown stood, smiled, and looked squarely at Wattles and then at Montgomery. "My friends," he started. "This is our last meeting. I go to prepare the way for freedom. I shall not live to see the work accomplished, but you shall both live to see the nations of the earth bless me and sing my praises. I leave with you these papers for future use, when, in your judgment the proper time shall have come."[1]

He reached out and handed Montgomery the bundle of papers that included the maps, list of men, and notes that had been gathered. Montgomery accepted them and looked down to avoid eye contact. "Farewell, friends," Brown said. He shook hands with Montgomery and then Wattles. Then he walked out of the room and to the front door. From there, he headed north.

He was correct. That was the last time he ever saw either of the two men face-to-face, though they continued to correspond through letters. When Brown was captured and jailed in Charlestown, Wattles, Montgomery, and two other men met at the Moneka Hotel to brainstorm ways to break

Brown out of jail. They could not come to an agreement. Montgomery and the others wanted a grand show of strength, at least 100 men to rain down an assault on the jail, but Wattles disagreed with that plan, considering it to be impractical.[2] Wattles thought a smaller, well-coordinated strike based on deception and meticulous orchestration would be a better approach. Somewhere in the middle, they reached an agreement, but when scouts were sent to tell Brown of the plan, he called off the delegation, preferring to die a martyr on the gallows instead.

Later, when Wattles was called to testify in front of Congress about his role in knowing about the raid at Harpers Ferry, he denied ever having known anything about the plan.

Establishing Home Base (July 3, 1859)

In 1852, Dr. Robert "Booth" F. Kennedy bought 194 acres in Washington County in southern Maryland from Antietam Iron Works. Chestnut Grove Road cut through the area, and not far off the road there was a small cottage in which Dr. Kennedy settled. He initially made the purchase as an investment property, but he grew attracted to the area and wanted to make the collier cabin his home. First, he built the story-high, stone foundation so that the one-room cabin could be raised to sit on it. The cabin had a loft over the single room, and that became the kitchen with an iron cookstove and a single door opening out onto the porch.

Next, he put a two-story addition onto the northeast backside of it, and that could be accessed through a door on the porch. It was made of logs that were hewn and joined with inverted V notches, and the gable end of the house were covered with random-width beaded boards.[3] It was secluded and fenced off for privacy, and Dr. Kennedy used the property until he died seven years later.

It was the privacy that the structure offered and the proximity to Harpers Ferry that caught Brown's attention as he was searching for somewhere that he could call headquarters. The house sat vacant and the acreage unproductive ever since Kennedy's death, so when a Mr. Isaac Smith, who said he was a cattle buyer from New York, came around looking for a place to rent, Booth's widow, the trustee of the estate, was willing to strike a deal. Mrs. Kennedy's attorney and Mr. Smith settled on an eight-month lease with the option to buy. They settled on $35 a month, and Smith paid the rent in gold. For his money, he got the old farmhouse, the pasture, the gardens surrounding the property, and a supply of firewood.

Moving in with Brown was his sixteen-year-old daughter Annie and his seventeen-year-old daughter-in-law Martha, who was married to his son, Oliver. Soon, Brown assembled his provisional army, recruiting twenty other willing participants. Some of the enlisted were physically and mentally more able than others, and some were difficult to get along with in such close quarters. It was about a three-and-a-half-month period that they suffered through humidly hot days, cold nights, and extremely cramped cohabitation in the farmhouse.

A stone fireplace was part of the larger log extension that was built over the rest to tie the original cabin to the additions. The fireplace appeared to support a living room at one time for Kennedy, but Brown used it as storage because no interior stairs connected the ground floor to that main floor section. Ascending the steps on the porch and entering the door of the main level, there were three small rooms. One room was the kitchen, which used to be the cabin, another room was both a dining and living room, and the backroom from the dining room was Martha and Annie's bedroom.[4]

Above the main floor was an attic. It was large but not nearly large enough to house the various ages and body types of the seventeen to twenty men that slept there, depending on the night. There were times when some would be away on duty or returned home to keep appearances and minimize questions and suspicion.

They used the basement areas to store the weapons out of sight from the occasional visitors. Shipments of pistols and rifles for the men arrived, and the pikes for the slaves came under the cover of night. The carriages would be quickly unloaded and sent back on their way to New York or Connecticut, where the pikes were being produced under contract.

Still playing the role of Isaac Smith, Brown also rented a room at Mary Ritner's boarding house on East King Street in Chambersburg. He had grown the infamous white beard as a disguise and spent time between the boarding house and the Kennedy farmhouse. His story was different to what he used in Maryland. In Chambersburg, he was known as a developer of iron mines in Maryland and Virginia. Crates began arriving in Chambersburg warehouses marked "mining implements," and from there, these crates would make their way to the farmhouse.

John Kagi was also planted in a boarding house in town, and he coordinated shipments as the middle passage, laundering the business to shield the operations at the farmhouse. The three Brown boys—Owen, Watson, and Oliver—were at the farmhouse to receive, unload, and store the freight. Along with weapons, ordinary supplies had to be transported. Three meals a day for twenty-five people took much planning with a regular stream of food being sent in because of the lack of storage space. Since the farmhouse sat vacant and empty after Dr. Kennedy's death, there was needed furniture, kitchenware, and everyday supplies to keep the grounds functioning. Along with the stream of commonplace deliveries for daily living that were shipped, there was of course, the many chests of rifles, pistols, and pikes.

During this time, the Old Captain, as he was also called in Anderson's book, exhausted himself by traveling night and day the 50 miles between the farm and Chambersburg. According to Anderson, he sometimes used his old brown mule, Dolly, and other times he would travel in his wagon. He would start directly after night and travel the 50 miles between the farm and Chambersburg by daylight next morning.[5]

The Middle Passage (July 1859)

In a letter sent from John Brown to the "War Secretary" John Kagi, dated July 12, 1859, Brown made it known that headquarters were established. A small farm said to be about 5 miles from Harpers Ferry was being rented under Brown's alias, Isaac Smith. Kagi cast a wide net and wrote over 100 letters fishing for men willing to take up arms and battle a government that would endorse social barbarity.

They waited patiently yet intently. Brown's vision of an army began to diminish as recruits dribbled into Chambersburg. There they waited at widow Mary A. Ritner's boarding house until Owen or Oliver (Brown's sons) brought the wagon to pick up another load of "tools."[6] From there, they would ride to the farmhouse.

Four Kansas raiders arrived about the same time—provisional army Captains Aaron D. Stevens and Charles Plummer Tidd and Lieutenants William H. Leeman and Albert Hazlett.[7]

Hazlett Gets the Message He Had Been Waiting For (March–July 1859)

When Albert returned to the homestead in Indiana, Pennsylvania, from Prescott, Kansas, he was a changed young man. Physically, he had gone through that late-teen growth spurt and his lanky frame grew a bit thicker. It was obvious to his mother that he had been putting in the work on his brother's farm. His shoulders were broadened with muscle, and his chest and stomach tapered down into a thin waistline, yet his personality was different, too.

The gruesome violence that he witnessed would chill the hardest of war veterans. While bloodshed and tyranny may frighten some, he seemed to be emboldened and even more committed to the cause of abolishing slavery.

He not only believed in the cause, but he believed in the methods. He believed in John Brown. He agreed with his mentors that violence was the answer, and the words and speeches of James Montgomery and John Brown consistently rang in his head while he did his routine chores, like feeding the chickens, repairing the fencing (which was a never-ending job), or even when relaxing on his mother's porch.

His father, a well-known stonemason in the wide-ranging area, had died in May 1856, and his mother, Sarah Miller of Bedford County, welcomed her son home with open arms, though he was strangely quiet. He walked the family's 50 acres silently and broodingly, obviously carrying with him an inner turmoil. He was growing impatient with Brown and sent him a letter that May to reinforce the fact that he was eager and ready.

As it was often the case during harvest time, neighbors asked each other to help with the harvesting. With fall quickly approaching, James Morrow Campbell asked Albert if he could help him with his harvest. "I will be glad to help," he replied, "but I must tell you that I am expecting a letter and when it would come, I must obey its summons."[8]

Mr. Campbell was happy to get any help that he could and said that whenever he must go, that he could just go. He underestimated the urgency in which Albert would react because he figured that he would at least finish what he started for that day.

Every morning before leaving the house to help Mr. Campbell on his farm, Albert kissed his mother goodbye and took his satchel packed with his entire earthly belongings along with him to put in the day's work in the field, always ready to leave Indiana at a moment's notice.

Then, it happened. One day, when Campbell was at the opposite end of the field, a messenger came to Hazlett. Hazlett made for his satchel and then went away, starting on a half run.[9] He never said goodbye to Mr. Campbell or gave the farmer a chance to thank him for his work. Hazlett was part of the first batch of men to report for duty, but it was not long after that others began showing up at the Kennedy Farm.

From Brown's hometown of North Elba, New York, Captain Watson Brown left his wife and newborn baby and teamed up with his father to help the insurgents. He brought his brothers-in-law William and Dauphin Thompson; both were easily recruited because they were unhappy in their position in the Adirondacks, and the two families built a strong bond as neighbors. The Thompsons joined the fight without the conviction and hatred for slavery that was characteristic of the others. From Springdale, Iowa, came two Quakers—Barclay and Edwin Coppoc, brothers who felt guilty for having forsaken their religious vows to not carry arms. Brown had persuaded them that God granted redemption to those who brought weapons of deliverance against the evils of slavery.[10]

Kagi's call to Canada proved fruitful for Osborne Anderson, a black man who was called a "mulatto" in his day and worked as a printer. It was not until October that two other free black Ohioans, John A. Copeland and his uncle Lewis Leary, answered the call and united with the others at Kennedy Farm, never to see their loved ones in Oberlin again.

Captain Cook recruited Dangerfield Newby, but when he showed up, Brown looked him over, evaluated his age and usefulness, and then dismissed the man and told him to return home. "Please, sah," Newby pleaded, "I's nothing to lose. Mah massa needs money and i' selling mah wife, Harriet, off, sah. They's ah plantation in L'isiana tha's gon' buy off mah wife and some o mah kids. Theys eight o em, but I loves dem all da same. I will fight to keep dem, sah. Please, sah, let me join your ahmy."

Brown furrowed his brow and focused those powerful blue eyes on him like a laser. "Not only will I be honored to have you join my provisional army," he started. "I will do you one better, sir. I promise that we will rescue your wife and children as soon as we empty the federal arsenal and arm volunteers to join us in freeing all slaves."

Time Spent at the Farmhouse (July–October 1859)

Albert looked deep into his fiery blue eyes, and he was drawn into Brown's words through a speech pattern that gave the feeling of earnestness and piety. He spoke ardently, "People will believe a complex lie over the simple truth. Politicians will tell you exactly what you want to hear but it will all be lies. Because you want to believe the lie. They say, 'Kansas will remain a free state.'" He growled from deep down in his gut, "Lies!" Brown continued:

> An eye for an eye. A tooth for a tooth. The bible teaches it, and God ordains it. Evil must be met with a fury that brings blood. If one more state turns to the dark side of evil and allows the heinousness of slavery, war will be the ultimate result because how can a sane and civilized society condone brutality for the sake of money? Capitalism begets greed, and greed is a sin; therefore, capitalism is sinful. The South brings us a greed and a scourge that needs [to be] repaired and reprimanded.
>
> The curse of the Dred Scott Decision, the ugliness of bondage for monetary gain, the blind eye given to villainy is on every American's head and hearts. I have been ordained and called upon by God himself to vanquish slavery and to right the wrongs of this nation. He has told me to expect a battle. He has told me that violence is the ultimate answer. This is not for the faint of heart, the weak of body or mind, the squeamish. This is the work that requires heroes. God granted heroes.

> States' rights. Bah! States' rights. Bah! Bah! When do men's rights become as protected as states' rights? When do we protect the rights bestowed to every man, woman, and child by God? States' rights do not supersede God's rights.

He spoke of it often. His men have heard the story over and over, so much so that it almost seemed to be their memory, their story.

> If you were brought up like me, if there was work to be done, you just did it. It didn't matter how old you were. I was 10 when I had to travel long distances, moving cattle, making deals with guys three times my elder. Coupled with the fact that the Bible tells us that it is a sin to own another human being, and degrade them with brutality, I despise the laziness of our Southern brethren. Sloth is a sin.
>
> On one of my travels in Michigan, I was graced with the hospitality of a gentleman that provided regular sup and cot. I was offered the kindness of the gentleman, and he had a young Negro slave that I got to know. The boy was about 10, 11, no more than 12, and though we may have been about the same age, we were treated very differently by the slave owner.
>
> He heaped praise on me for being so mature and such a hard cattle driver, but the poor boy was beaten regularly with household tools or anything within reach. He'd yell at the boy, attempting to crush his spirit. He'd make the boy sleep in the cold barn in mere rags. Then one day the boy made a minor error. What it was I don't remember, something trivial, but I do remember the disapproval of his slaveholder. The savage brute grabbed the first instrument at hand, which happened to be an iron fire shovel, and he beat that poor boy within inches of his life.

Brown paused at this point and stared at the ground nearly every time he told the story because it is what happens next that seemed to shock Brown the most.

> The man calmly returns the shovel to its resting place, sits back down, and continues to finish his dinner, as evenly as if he had just put on his boots. I never returned to that house again, so I don't know how that pitiful Negro fared. I pray to God that he healed. I pray that he was not permanently maimed; however, the blunt force of the iron shovel and the sound of it upon his skull suggested that the boy was going to die. If he didn't die, surely his life was changed and made more difficult.
>
> I had seen the horrors of slavery, and I feared it. I empathized with that boy and wanted so much to do something for him, but I couldn't figure out what I could do. I felt helpless.

There were times when the story would stop there, and then there were times when Brown would go on to further illuminate his development of when he found the answer to combat slavery directly.

> I had a close friend and mentor named Reverend Elijah P. Lovejoy. Reverend Lovejoy was a brilliant man, and he was a Presbyterian minister and an editor of an abolitionist newspaper in Illinois. Do you know how some people just seem to connect with you and speak to you like no other? That was him to me. His words against slavery were an inspiration to me and touched me deeply.
>
> Then, one night a proslavery mob from St. Louis made their way to his hometown of Alton and destroyed Reverend Lovejoy's printing press and operation. He tried to fight them off, but he was murdered in the process. When I heard the news of his death, I told myself, right then and there, that by God and all things holy, I was going to cure that which had diseased our country. This plague, this scourge, this abomination against mankind was going to be ended by none other than me.
>
> At his funeral, he was shown to be loved by many. There were a host of speakers, but I was not to be one of them. I sat silently in the back of the room. However, I got up that day, raised my right hand up to God, and declared, "Here before God, in the presence of these witnesses, from this time, I consecrate my life to the destruction of slavery."[11]

In the evenings before he went to bed and the men got prepared to move about through the night to avoid the neighbors, he would tell stories. Mainly, they were anecdotes with morals or just stories of him lamenting about his family and being a father.

> My grandfather fought in the Revolutionary War because he believed in freedom and liberty. He fought against oppression not because he wanted to see us enslave the Negro but because he wanted to see America grow into a strong enough nation that will allow the individual to grow to his full potential.
>
> My grandfather lived to be a ripe old-timer, all the while raising my father to believe in the exact same ideals that he believed in, and he, in turn, raised me with the same. And, how do you think I raised my children?

He would look for one of his children to ask them, and usually one of them was around because they followed him closely. Sometimes, it would be one of the boys, who usually sat and played cards at his side, but other times, it would be one of the girls tending to him. "My love," he said at this time to get the attention of his daughter, "how did I raise you?" She answered:

> My father had solemnly pledged himself, and our entire family took the vow with him, to do everything and suffer everything to wipe out slavery.[12]
>
> John Brown is the most humane, tender, loving, and just of men. I have known him to sit up all night to nurse a sick lamb, and no suffering creature but claimed a share of his compassion. It is this trait of his character that makes him hate slavery so intensely, for he had witnessed the awful sufferings of slave women from whom their children had been separated and had seen strong men writhe under the lash.[13]

Brown replied:

> Thank you, my love. After my wife died when my children were young, raising them became my sole duty, and in raising my children I have never spared the rod, either. I raised my children close to God and sin was punished. Once my little beloved Ruth, went wading out into the mud to retrieve some pussy-willows. Her boots were covered in mud, and when I asked her how she came to be so muddy and why she tracked mud all through the house, she initially was not purely honest with me in her answers; therefore, later that night when her work was done, I tenderly and kindly explained her misdeeds and took the willow branches that she brought into the house and used them against her while putting her over my knee. Lying was abhorred and not tolerated in my house.
>
> On another occasion, my loyal son John was helping out in the tannery while I worked at the Government's post office. John at the time could be lazy, like most children, and sloth is a sin that eats slowly at one's soul. John helped to grind the bark but was often rather idle. I noted his faults, idleness, various disobediences, and omissions, and all were added to the list. I had given him fair warning that these notations were being made and that they would build until a debt needed [to be] collected. So, one day, I called together some of the children, Jason, Owen, Ruth to follow John and I into the woods to witness his "reckoning up."[14] I went and prepared a switch, and the children stood with their heads cast at the ground, John's feet sullenly twiddling.
>
> I went on and explained to the children the importance of faithfulness in the small matters of life, the moral result of disobedience, and my own love for him that led me to the use of the rod. I stripped off my shirt, got down on one knee, and said, "And now, son, there are twenty-five lashes due you, but I will take them in your stead. When you know that

> I suffer in body as well as mind for your faults, perhaps you will be more careful."[15]
>
> I put the "instrument of torture" in John's hand and implored him to whip me for his sins. At first, he was very gentle, not wanting to hurt his poor father, but after I implored and compelled him to strike harder, he cried, and the other children shrieked as John laid on the whip.[16]

Yet, another story that Brown loved to tell was the day he left his church in Ohio. He would set the story up by identifying the sermon topics given on Sunday mornings.

> They talk of peace, harmony, and understanding. They give elaborate sermons on the importance of unity, sanctity, and being followers of Christ. And, then you turn around and see that there is a Negro section in the back of the church.
>
> Well, one Sunday morning, there was only one Negro family there in the back pew, isolated from the rest of the congregation. I thought it only right that they should come worship with the rest of us, so I went back to the family and told them to follow me up to my pew to sit with my family, you know, togetherness.
>
> After the sermon, I was called into the Deacon's office to be reprimanded for my actions, and there he went on to explain that I wasn't to break the rules of the church, Negroes in the back, white people up front. Those were the norms. I told him that it made no sense to me and that we are all God's children to worship together. He gave me an ultimatum. He said either I follow the rules, or I wasn't welcomed at the church anymore. So, I told the great Deacon that he had seen the last of me, and I went on to worship elsewhere.

Douglass Warns Brown (August 16, 1859)

Frederick Douglas visited Chambersburg and gave a speech at the Franklin Repository by the courthouse and town square. After the speech, he was approached by Henry Watson, a barber and local agent on the Underground Railroad. Watson took Douglass and his accomplice, Shields Green, to meet John Brown, where he and Kagi were fishing in the Conococheague. Knowing how jumpy the old man could be, they approached him cautiously. Douglass noticed that Brown was as tired and worn as his beaten hat. Douglass, Kagi, Brown, and Green sat down among the rocks and talked over the enterprise that was about to be undertaken.[17]

"With what you represent to the Negro, together, we could cut a path through the south to send shockwaves of terror," Brown said.

"You can't believe that our government, in all its power, would allow you to get away with such a coup, do you?" Douglass asked of the plan.

"As powerful as our government is, God is more powerful. God has called on me to pull this off in the face of our government, to end this evilness and forgive us our sin."

"But my fight is with words, not with guns."[18]

"Words will not stop slavery. If they could, they would have already. Peace won't end a war on our values or humanity, only violence and bloodshed will do that. I guess, if you do not have the stomach for that, sir, then it is probably best that you return home. Return to your war of words."

Douglass felt for Brown and understood how painful empathy and compassion could be. "Please reconsider, John," he said. "This is a suicide mission that pushes to the limits of insanity. In fact, I am certain that insane may be the best description of this mission." The Old Man stared as if in disbelief that Douglass did not wholeheartedly join the fight. He said nothing.

"John, you are stepping into a perfect steel trap,"Douglass pleaded.[19]

"The very weakness of geography and the terrain is its strength," Brown said. "We come down through the mountain to the bottom of the bowl, seize the armory and take its contents, and then come back out of the bowl in the cover the mountains provide. The mountains stretch forth into the South like a long arm of freedom and will conceal the Negro in a vast embrace of trees and hidden places."[20]

"I'm sorry, John. There are better ways to combat evil. Love. Peacefulness. Reason and rationality. They already see us Negroes as savages. I don't want to be the savage that they expect and fear. Do as you must, but understand, that you will do it without me. I will help you in any other way that I can, but I can't take part in this."

Brown grabbed his hand and held it as he said, "I understand. I could never think less of you. I understand that this task is not for everyone, that's why I feel like I've been chosen for this. I was born for this. Who am I to deny God's destiny for me?"

Feeling the conversation over at a stalemate, Douglass turned to Shields and asked, "Are you about ready to go on to Rochester with me?"

Shields stood still, and his inaction to gather to leave took Douglass by surprise. "I b'leve I'll go wid de ol' man," Green said coolly.[21]

The Nosey Neighbor (Early August–October 1859)

Life on the farm was burdensome and boring. The summer nights in the attic were unbearable. After the sun beat on the roof, hillside, and exposed outcrops all day, the heat escaped and rose in the evenings, putting off a stifling sweat-inducing energy. The humidity gave a greenhouse effect that made some nights almost impossible to sleep in the cramped quarters.

Annie, the younger of the two sisters, used the blazing summer sun to dry the laundry, making sure to put out a little at a time in case the two nosey neighbors would unexpectedly stop by for an impromptu visit.

There were times when the men would attempt to spend some time out of the attic, and the nosy neighbors from down the street, Ms. Nichols or Mrs. Elizabeth Huffmaster, would stop by to check up on the women of the house and spend time chatting. Each time they would sneak up on the men, they would narrowly escape the women's view. It always seemed like they suspected something, asking a lot of questions and popping up time and time again as to catch them with their guard down.

"Oh, hello, Mrs. Huffmaster," Annie said answering the door.

"I brought over some butter that we churned. Is your father home? I'd like to give it to him."

"No, Pa and the boys went off hunting. I will tell him that you dropped off the butter, so in return, you wait right here." Annie disappeared into the kitchen and returned to the front door. "Pa wanted me to give this to you and your four little darlings." She handed her some milk and salted meats.

"Oh, I couldn't," Mrs. Huffmaster feigned. Annie reached out and gave the oldest child, who was eight, a bundle and put the milk jug in Mrs. Huffmaster's hand. "I am ever so humbled," she said accepting the gifts while batting her eyes.

The way the houses were situated, the Huffmaster's had a good view of the outside stairway that had to be used to get to the second floor of the Kennedy Farm.[22] If there was anyone suspecting mischief at the farmhouse, it was Mrs. Huffmaster, a thirty-three-year-old woman with four young girls and married to a laborer. According to both Brown girls in their writings, Mrs. Huffmaster caught glimpses of the guys with her unexpected visits. She even saw Annie with Albert and a couple of the guys sitting around the kitchen table together.

However, the more she suspected, the more she played along. She began bribing the Browns, covertly asking for gifts and wanting to be appeased because of her tough questioning. As the summer passed and fall approaching, Mrs. Huffmaster grew bolder and sneakier with her visits.

On one occasion, she opened the door while knocking and calling, "Oh, Annie. Annie darling, do you happen to ha-" she stopped short, shocked by the presence of Shields Green in the front room. Annie came running to the door and caught Mrs. Huffmaster and pushed her back outside while closing the door behind her.

"Annie, there's a nigger standing in your house," Mrs. Huffmaster said in shock. "Are you harboring runaway slaves, Annie? Is that what you people moved in here to do?"

"No, ma'am, he is a free man visiting here with some friends."

"What your father chooses to do is his business," Mrs. Huffmaster said, "but be warned, this is not New York. This is not even Pennsylvania, where I'm from. This is Maryland, and harboring slaves here is serious business." She said no more and left. Annie did not know how to interpret the situation.

When her father arrived, she recounted the story in a panic. "Well," her father said, "no authorities came to the property since the encounter. She could be a spy, just laying low and watching the place."

"I don't think she is any more than a little hen with her chickens," Annie said.[23] "She is a plague and a torment, but I think that she is quite harmless."[24]

"Well, just keep an eye out," her father commanded, "and, please, I know that you can, so will you somehow fix this problem?"

"Yes, father, I know how to handle her and her brood of little ones. They are always in want of something. Gifts should take care of this."

As predicted, the more Annie gave Mrs. Huffmaster, the more she asked for, even if she did have suspicions about "Isaac Smith" and his family aiding fugitives from slavery. It is possible that Huffmaster was sympathetic. Although the wife of a Maryland man and Pennsylvania born, it is possible she had no great desire either to help or hinder black people—a common attitude among northern white people in the antebellum era.[25]

It was probably thanks to Mrs. Huffmaster that Isaac Smith earned a reputation throughout the community as a kind, generous, and well-respected Christian man, as a general assessment. Brown was well-liked by those who knew him. At his homes in New York, Pennsylvania, and Kansas, Brown was viewed as a caring, giving, and spiritual man, offering his services in any way that he could.

As it was, Mrs. Huffmaster had a growth on her neck that was obviously maligning her. She conscientiously dressed to hide it and turned away when she felt it causing attention when talking with anyone. It was a nuisance that undermined her confidence, and as she felt, distracted from her beauty. Apparently, she had suffered with it for some time before

Brown offered to perform the operation that would extract the tumor. Brown was not a queasy, delicate sort, either, and one can almost imagine the confidence and gentleness that accompanied this procedure: with tools carefully prepared and the woman biting down on leather to fend off the pain, the Old Man, assisted by Annie and Martha, cut out the tumor from the flesh of Mrs. Huffmaster, then sewed up the bloody wound as she cried and groaned—the hidden raiders listening the whole time from upstairs.[26]

The Plan Gets Sabotaged in the Fourth Quarter (September and October 1859)

The older men spent the time talking, resting, and thinking. They took the downtime as if it were time to recharge their batteries and save their strength for the battle that was to come. They practiced, rehearsed, and visualized the plan. Though they had the patience and tenacity to spend hours of ennui occupying their mind, the younger men like Hazlett and Leeman drove themselves crazy with boredom.

At times, gifts would arrive to honor those who reported for duty. Supporters would send the men treats, snacks, or weaponry through Brown. One crate arrived filled with purple woolen blankets from a group in Philadelphia. A Mrs. Adams wrote Brown and told him that the blankets could double as coats or blankets. They were monogrammed for the men, and Hazlett's came with an E. H. for "Elbert Hazlett." The shawls came in handy as the men marched into Harpers Ferry, for they draped them over their shoulders to protect their Sharps rifle from the rain. Later, though, witnesses made mention of them as identifiers, and the existence of their tattered fragments in the graves were later used as confirmation that the right coffins were located.

Sometimes, to get out, Hazlett and Leeman would sneak down to the river to do some fishing, and even on extreme occasions, they snuck into Harpers Ferry to look up Captain Cook, who was positioned there long-term to infiltrate the town. On these occasions, they would supplement the leisure trip with practical usefulness for they would act as messengers to report back and pass on any news from Cook to the Old Man.

The men played cards and checkers. Some of them read; however, not all were totally literate; even still, they all would argue with capability about the most mundane topics. They learned how to push each other's buttons and knew the exact words to start debate or escalate a situation. They dedicated a considerable amount of time to drilling maneuvers, studying and discussing guerrilla warfare tactics, and exercising to build their endurance. They conditioned themselves to a more nocturnal lifestyle.

Sleeping most of the day and becoming more active in the early evenings on through the night. In the early mornings, they would retreat into the attic and settle in for the day.

It was always Brown's belief that he would recruit hundreds of men, if not thousands. The number of arms in possession and part of the overall plan suggested that notion. At the farm were 200 breech-loading 0.52-caliber Sharps carbines and at least 950 pikes, and there were known to be over 100,000 muskets and rifles at the armory, which was a large complex targeted to be seized and its contents distributed.

He had a genuine conviction that the movement would snowball into great numbers, so he thought the idea to be an easy sell. Those who were susceptible to grand schemes and heartfelt pitches were primed for Brown. Riding the wave of vogue intellectualism and Great American thought that questioned the system of slavery, like Henry David Thoreau, Walt Whitman, Nathaniel Hawthorne, and Oliver Wendell Holmes, Brown's philosophies and beliefs were slowly becoming the fashion and consciousness of the nation.

Since the episode of "Bleeding Kansas" and the brutal force displayed there, there seemed to be a growing tide and intolerance for slavery and a growing tolerance for the idea of violence to end it. Pro-slavery opposition and stubbornness brought an acceptance of violence and chaos as a means to combat it. To be able to arm a large group seemed to be easy to Brown, thus he began rounding up all the axiomatic carts before the horses.

Thanks to some wealthy backers, known as the Secret Six, Brown was able to get funding for his plan, and though they took the precaution to make sure that they were not tied to Brown or any of his plans, they were aware of what was right on the horizon. For centuries, America turned a blind eye, but now people were seeing how they could chip in to end slavery.

There were the naysayers, of course, and one became dangerously outspoken. The well-known and admired British veteran of the Italian wars, Hugh Forbes, tried to warn Brown's backers and convince them that Brown's plan was tactically unsound and that they should pull funding.

Forbes tried to convince Brown that small, silent, guerrilla-style pop shots were the best strategy. Instead of the violent and chaotic ambushes employed by Brown in Kansas, Forbes thought that raiding farms and allowing slaves to escape in large numbers would undermine the reliability of the institutions and focus on the fact that freedom was more of an impulse, making the institution of slavery too unreliable.[27] When he saw Brown disregarding his opinions, Forbes began turning on him.

Forbes viewed Brown as a delusional zealot embarking on a plan that had no chance without talented and trained staff, regardless of Brown's insistence that God had ordained it. By the same token, there was no love lost, for

Forbes was losing respect in the raiders' eyes. While the men at Kennedy Farm read and studied Forbes' manual that he wrote in 1855, *Manual for the Patriotic Volunteer on Active Service in Regular and Irregular War*, and another pamphlet that he wrote called "Duties of a Soldier," which sold Brown on this very idea while he was in Kansas, their respect for Forbes and his opinion waned. He was unpredictable and his reputation as a down-and-out drunk on Delancey Street did nothing for his credibility.

Forbes wrote, "Right is that which is good true honorable just human self-sacrificing—it is the opposite of wrong."[28] Not only did all the men subscribed to this notion, it was a cornerstone belief. Another belief that all had in common was the wrongness of slavery, even though Forbes did not share Brown's unyielding belief in the equality of races.[29]

Brown and Forbes had a negative history with their connection being strained ever since Brown hired him to help train an army of men in Kansas and Iowa. The two met in 1857 when Forbes was making ends meet by teaching fencing lesson in New York and translating and editing for *The European* and writing for *The New York Tribune,* so the soldier of fortune was anxious to find work doing what he loved best, warfare. Forbes felt that he was lied to and sold a bill of goods when he reported to duty in Tabor, Iowa, and found no army but Brown and his sons. Waiting for more to come for training, Forbes stuck around to help with the planning in Harpers Ferry. As time passed, he grew more and more frustrated with Brown. He wanted to be paid for his time and was ready to leave Tabor. He left unpaid.

Of course, Forbes was irritated that he did not get paid, yet the only other alternative was getting guys recruited to meet in Ohio for training and finally get monetary reimbursement. When he showed up in Ohio to the same scenario and no pay, Forbes got mad and started soiling Brown's name, warning his investors of Brown's crazy scheme and the inevitable failure of it. Brown wanted to get the plan up and running sooner than later, but because of Forbes, the affair had to be delayed and more traveling and letters was necessary to make visits to re-sell the endeavor and restore confidence.

Brown did not waste time during the delay that Forbes' badmouthing caused. He made more contacts and landed a better recruiter in Kagi, who personally wrote over 100 individuals to join in the crusade. Then Brown dispatched Cook and other lookouts to gather better information in Harpers Ferry and Carlisle. He purchased maps of Harpers Ferry, scouted locations for storage and other various needs, and made deals for weapons.

Forbes wanted no parts of this raid, yet he was implicated when his books were gathered as evidence back at the farmhouse in the wake of the demise of the venture. Notes, maps, and other belongings that were confiscated suggested the small number of men who wanted to pull off a Spartan type of victory. When it came to light that Forbes also tipped off Senators Wilson and Seward, he slipped off into obscurity. Either in a drunken rage, a legitimate concern for those involved, a strange jealousy, or sheer ignorance, Forbes set into motion the failure of the plan early that spring.

On the contrary, Brown and the men did not consider failure as an option. The way they saw it, if all men were killed there on the spot, they would get an immense amount of attention and perhaps spur someone after them to rally their cause. If they were successful, like they supposed, they would trigger a crusade that would end slavery and all the ugliness that it stood for.

That is why they vigilantly trained, suffered hot days and nights in an attic, spent hours upon hours held up in the farmhouse like hostages, and made other sacrifices because they believed in Brown and his plan, and they committed themselves to its success.

9

The Development of a Soldier

Hazlett's Early Years to Leaving Home as a Young Man (Spring 1857)

With coal mining and the railroad system, Indiana became known as a bustling town. The borough of Indiana essentially grew overnight since its inception in 1816. People who lived in the area saw rapid growth in their lifetimes, thanks to the surrounding company patch towns, whose sole economic purpose and dependency was on the coal industry. For years, farming and service trades were the backbone of the economy, but in 1846, the Pennsylvania legislature chartered the Pennsylvania Railroad Company, headquartered in Philadelphia to build a connection between Harrisburg to Pittsburgh. Two years later, the first passenger train ran from Philadelphia to Pittsburgh with Indiana being a key stop along the route.

In addition, soft bituminous coal made mining by hand easier but more dangerous. The first mine broke ground in 1760 at Coal Hill, which is today's Mount Washington in Pittsburgh. Coal manufacturing had close to a hundred years of growth to the point that coal was king in western Pennsylvania, so by the time Albert was a teen, Indiana County became a destination for European immigrant workers occupying homes provided by coal companies and creating their own towns. These "patch towns," where companies built their own settlements to either mine coal or build coke ovens to meet the high demand from the booming steel industry, were scattered throughout the entire region, but to get a taste of life outside of the company, Indiana was the landing place.

Albert's grandfather, William Hazlett, moved from Bedford to about 2 miles west of Mechanicsburg in 1825. They were said to be quiet and deeply religious.[1] He raised seven children—John, Moses, Mary McKane, Nancy Barlow, Barbara Farrier, and Alexander.

Alexander married Sarah Miller of Bedford, and they had nine children—John, William, Jonas, Peter, Absalom, Jerry, Henry, Mary Ann, and Sara, who died in childhood. Alexander was a stonemason, who bounced around from place to place until his sister, Mary McKane, died and willed him a 50-acre farm. He lived there and worked the farm until his death in 1856.

In Absalom's formative years, he preferred the name "Albert" and asked everyone to call him by that name. Living on the farm and going into town seemed like a mini-vacation for Albert as a kid. He was fascinated by the people who all seemed in a rush to go somewhere. He noticed the way people with money carried themselves. They had fine clothes, a different attitude and vibe, and a different way of walking. Even rich older people walked upright, their backs not hunched, and their knees not buckled from years of carrying or heaving heavy things. They were refined, spoke well, and their hair was neatly cut. Albert's mother and father encouraged, if not enforced, a certain amount of refinement. On the farm, he had to show dignity and respect to his parents and siblings by speaking to them a certain way, and they most certainly had to be well-groomed in all aspects at home. The difference, however, was a noticeable metropolitan sophistication.

He and his brothers would either walk the tracks or hop a train to town, which was just about a 2-mile trek. Hopping a train was a rush because it was such risky business, but the boys felt that if they could run along the side of it without losing pace, they could hop it. There were even times when his older brothers would make it on, but he could not. "See ya at the station," they would laugh and holler.

Soon, the older boys moved on from the house to stake their own claims, and then there were only the two youngest, Albert and Jonas. Though Jonas was the older of the two, they could serve as twins at first glance. They were mistaken for one another all the time by people who saw them from a distance or were casual acquaintances of the family. As they had seen their older brothers do, they began moonlighting as porters on the weekends when their farm chores were done.

Taking passengers' bags from the main entrance gate to the baggage car, the boys worked for tips. The passenger station was on the northwest corner of Philadelphia Street. It was a wooden structure that saw travelers from the large cities of Philadelphia, Pittsburgh, and Harrisburg; on the north end of that, there was a brick structure that served as the freight station. The boys got good at spotting and approaching potential good tippers to carry their bags and trunks from the station to the hotel across the street—the Continental Hotel.

On the corner of Philadelphia Street and Eighth was a large residential property that was transformed into an inn as the town grew more commercial from the coal trade. In the summer of 1865, it was enlarged by Solomon Earhart, who added a story, and first opened it as a hotel, calling it the "Continental."[2]

Solomon and his brother, Martin, were originally from the town of Saltsburg, about 20 miles west of Indiana. Right outside of Indiana, which would now be Route 286 West, they had a livery stable business. Seeing the potential in the property for sale right across from the railroad station, Solomon purchased the property and began a profitable hotel that changed hands and names throughout history until it burned down in 1966 as the Moore Hotel.

Behind the hotel was the blacksmith shop called the Plow and Wagon Factory, and adjacent to that was Indiana Marble Works, who ran ads in the local paper boasting of marble or slate headstones at a "very low price."

As you entered the hotel, there was the check-in desk and off to the right of that was a cloakroom for those eating or sitting around and drinking at the bar. At seventeen and eighteen and never having an overcoat or seeing his father wear something so costly, Albert would walk by the coats sitting there and lament his plight of being raised on a farm.

By the time he was nineteen, Absalom no longer carried bags to the Continental, but he would hang out at the hotel to drink, talk politics, and flirt with girls at the hotel lounge. His brother, John, had been going back and forth between Prescott in Bourbon County, Kansas, and home in Indiana, purveying the opportunities. The promises of cheap land for those willing to till it encouraged westward expansion. Prescott was right on the state line bordering Missouri, and though tensions were mounting about states being designated Free States or Slave States, the land was fertile and primed for farming, at least that was the government's pitch to lure people to the region. John eventually made up his mind that he was going to move there and start anew. The oldest brother, William, had already settled in the area, and he wrote letters of how he and his new wife Elizabeth Fyock were thriving and happy in the area.

"Go West, Young Man, go west" was the mantra. "Grow up with your country," writer Horace Greeley said, and it resonated, especially with bright-eyed young Americans who were not afraid of hard work or the dangers of the unknown. There was a sense of duty and patriotism to conquering and cultivating the rugged west. It was based in virtue and spirituality. The mission was to redeem America and remake the west as a mirror image of the very foundations of the country's agrarian ideals. To Albert, it then made no sense that the country would introduce slavery to the uncorrupted ideals that the west represented.

"Why don't you come with me?" John asked. "With you, we could double our production."

"I don't know, John," Albert said with consternation. "What about Ma? I'll stick around and take care of the farm."

"Albert," John started with pity in his voice. "The farm is used up. It is now mostly clay and the soil is shot. It was not a great producer when Pa was alive, so now it certainly couldn't sustain you and Ma. You'll end up working ol' man Morrow's farm more than our own. Come to Kansas. Let's go west, young man," he grabbed a handful of Albert's shirt sleeve and gave him a little shake.

"I don't know, John. Let me think about it."

About a week later, John left for Kansas, and about a week after that, Albert got a letter from his brother asking him to reconsider. He was able to purchase some acreage with the pittance that he was able to save, along with the little bit his mother had given them from the family nest egg. He said he had already begun tilling and planting, so pulling the first harvest would not be that far off and that it would be great to work the harvest like old times. Albert liked the idea, but he was not willing to commit to the offer.

One night at the Continental's lounge, Albert was there laughing and drinking with some friends when before he even realized it, he had too much to drink. He laughed uncontrollably and talked louder than anyone in the lounge. Out of the corner of his eye, he could tell that some out-of-towners were watching him and his friends. They shook their heads and rolled their eyes in disgust of the drunken belligerence of Albert and his friends, and to spite, Albert began turning up his outrageousness another notch.

"One more round, barkeeper," Albert shouted down the bar. "I'm not paying, but one more round for everybody," he laughed and slapped the bar.

"Ah," the bartender started to object, "I'm afraid you may have had enough tonight, sir."

"Are you kidding me?" Albert said. "As much as I come in here! You're cutting me off! This is ridiculous. Get Mike. Where's Mike?"

"It's late, sir. Mike is gone for the day."

"Albert, Albert," his friends said pulling at him.

Another friend agreed, "Yeah, it's okay. It's alright. We're done anyway. I gotta get home before Betsy skins me alive anyway. Let's call it a day. We'll do it again tomorrow." One by one, the small group of men finished their glasses and slid them to the bar rail, nodding to the bartender. They patted Albert on his back to say goodbye, and then headed out of the lounge. Albert could hear them still laughing and carrying on in the lobby as they exited the building.

Albert turned his attention back on the bartender. "What is your name?" he asked with malice in his voice. "You're new here. I've been coming here for years. Everybody knows me here. I've been schlepping bags and trunks around this hotel since I was a kid. Who the hell …"

"Listen, fella," one of the men interrupted from the table that had been watching the incident unfold. "Why don't you just go home, huh? Your buddies were right. The party's over. It is time to leave."

Albert glared at the men and knew deep down that they were right. Even through the drunken haze, he thought of his family's disappointment if they could see how vainly and obnoxiously he was acting. The men turned their attention away from him and began talking to each other. Albert could not hear what they were saying, but he was sure that he heard the word "redneck" in their discussion. He slunk out of the bar, humiliated.

Passing the cloakroom, he had an idea. He looked out at the check-in desk and saw that it was unmanned. It was getting late, so James, who usually closed in the evenings, had probably gone to tidy up the back, maybe even smoke a cigarette in his office, and be ready to walk out the door by closing time. Albert went into the cloakroom and sized up the most expensive overcoats hanging there. He pulled one with his left hand that he knew to be fine wool, and with his right, he grabbed the biggest armful that he could comfortably carry out of the hotel. He was cool and calculated as he left the cloakroom and calmly headed through the lobby with silk shawls and tweed and camel hair overcoats that the early spring nights call for in Western Pennsylvania.

He just about made it out the door when he heard someone call behind him, "Albert! What are you doing?" He made a run for it, knowing full well that he had been caught red-handed. He burst through the door, heading for the back alley to dump the coats and lighten the load to run faster, but he heard James at the front of the hotel, calling to the railroad policemen, who happened to be standing in front of the station. "Catch him! He's getting away with stealing coats from the lounge!"

A few moments later, he was tackled to the ground, roughed up, and hauled back to his feet. It was all a blur to him. While sitting in a holding cell at the town jailhouse, he remembered being knocked around and in the scuffle seeing James's blurry face and hearing him say, "Albert, how could you?"

Early the next morning, Albert was dragged before the magistrate. "You are being accused of drunk and disorderly conduct and stealing private property. You don't have to enter a plea this morning, but you are scheduled to appear before a judge. If you want to enter a guilty plea, your fines and penalty can be assessed this morning. Do you wish to enter a plea?" Albert continued to look at the floor without saying a word. "Do you understand the circumstances that I just laid out to you?" the magistrate asked.

Albert said nothing but gave a single nod of his head. "Okay, then," the magistrate started. "If you cannot afford counsel, the court will provide you with one. Otherwise, it is noted that you have refused to enter a plea, and your trial will be set for..." he trailed off, looking over his glasses and into a docket. "Your trial will ... be," he hesitated while scanning his papers, "set ... for," he paused, "how about April 2? That will give you about a month to get things in order for yourself. If you enter a guilty plea before that time, you will probably be looking at a misdemeanor and a fine. If you continue to poke your finger in the eye of the system and show contempt the way you are doing now after being caught red-handed, you could face a jail sentence. How's that? One last time, do you wish to enter a plea?"

Albert never made eye contact or made any type of motion. "Okay," the magistrate said. "You will be released on your own recognizances, and we will see you on April 2nd," he said. He waved Albert away and shouted, "Next!"

That night, Albert sat down at the dinner table beside an oil lamp and began writing a letter to John. "Good news!" it began, "I have decided to move out west with you and help you with the coming harvest." With that, before his trial date, he was gone.

Hazlett Joins James Montgomery's Army (Winter 1858)

There is no documentation anywhere to suggest that any of Absalom's brothers took part in any raids in Kansas with John Brown or James Montgomery, but there were suggestions that Albert was involved with anti-slave gangs, stints in Ohio, a horse-thieving ring, and other mischief prior to his permanent position in Kansas. Some assume that his brothers, John and Jonas also took part in anti-slavery raids and rebellions since they had the same religious upbringing, harbored the same convictions against the institution, were about the same age, and had the same interests and negative reputation as Albert.

John was settled in the area, and Jonas was known to pop up here and there without solid ties to any area, seemingly more of a free spirit. Jonas did frequently return to Indiana to stay with his mother periodically, probably more of a sense of duty than an attachment to a woman that had many children and long-lasting relationships with only a couple. A number of other brothers were believed to have moved into Kansas in the early 1860s, for the family had lost the farm by then.

By the time Absalom moved out to Prescott, Kansas, to stay with his brother, the name "James Montgomery" started carrying a great deal of weight throughout the territory. Did Absalom know of Montgomery before moving out to Kansas? Probably not, but given Albert's anti-slavery ideals, the circles he associated with, and his wayward tendencies, it could not have been long before he heard mention of his name from other local farmers that either feared him or revered him when gathered for drinks at the local tavern. Meeting Montgomery seemed inevitable.

In Kansas, agitated pro-slavery people were frustrated that their safety and property were not being protected because authorities seemed to turn a blind eye to the fear and mayhem the anti-slavery rebels were causing. They were determined to take matters into their own hands.

Hard and sugar maple trees made up the wooded hills that lined rolling, fertile valleys cut by serpentine streams. "Jayhawkers" was the term applied to anti-slavery people of Kansas, while pro-slavery Missourians were called "Bushwhackers." Tensions rose to such heights between the two factions that "Border Wars" and violence broke out in the years preceding the Civil War. Leading the charge for the Jayhawkers from his headquarters in Mound City, Kansas, was Charles R. Jennison, known as "Doc" Jennison, who later served as a Union colonel in the Civil War and was elected to the Kansas State Senate in the 1870s.

Living in Mound City since his unpleasant stay in Pike County, Missouri, was James Montgomery. Montgomery had a particular style and success in organizing men for a cause. He did not promise a participant's safety, but he could promise the benefit of the element of surprise. In quick bursts, Montgomery would organize and dispatch small bands of men to take weapons, horses, and rations from pro-slavery inhabitants. Boundary lines were still unclear from town to town and county to county, so the boundaries of jurisdiction, as far as the Territorial Militia under Governor John Geary was concerned, meant primarily nothing.

Prescott did not get its name until 1870. It was first called Coal Centre because coal was easily stripped and sent by railroad from the town, but when the post office was established on June 13, 1870, the name resembled other Kansas post office names; therefore, the town took on the name of the treasurer of the railroad company, C. H. Prescott.

About 10 to 15 miles from where Absalom and his brother John worked and tilled the land in Bourbon County, James Montgomery was establishing himself in Linn County, Kansas. Originally from Ohio, Montgomery was a tall and lanky man with a wiry beard and a long, thin nose. He is described by those who knew him well as a man of tranquility. He chose his words carefully and that made him a slow, methodical talker. Spiritually, he was a fundamentalist evangelical, deeply devoted and born again. To him, the Bible was God's Word to inspire humankind with the piety of perfect truth, and the Bible was the final authority in all matters of doctrine and faith. Though he believed that his salvation was his acceptance of Jesus Christ as his savior, he, too, believed that violence was a true and logical tool to combat evil. He saw slavery as evil.

While in Kansas, Montgomery was a minister and school teacher, and he became repulsed by the imposition of the staunch pro-slavery people that "popular sovereignty" brought flooding the area; therefore, Montgomery moved his family in 1854 to Jackson County, Missouri, which mirrored Mound City in Linn County, Kansas, that sprang up the following year. Trouble began instantly brewing in Mound City because pro-slavery settlers from South Carolina arrived in Bourbon County, just north of Linn County, and began causing trouble and intimidating those who disagreed with them. Their goal was to turn the state into a slave state by brute force and fear. Also, there were two organized groups, the Southern Emigrant Aid Society and the Dark Lantern Society, who funded a campaign to drive anti-slavery inhabitants either into silence or completely away.

In February 1855 at the Lecompton constitution vote, the very first convention in the county at Sugar Mound, now Mound City, Montgomery made a dramatic scene and broke the ballot box as a symbolic gesture that made the newspapers and received a little national attention. He was indicted but never brought to trial.[3]

By 1856, pro-slavery Kansans and Missourians ordered all anti-slavery sympathizers out of the area. At first, their orders were subtle. Then they grew more malevolent and threatening, and when verbal threats and warning shots did not work, the Bushwhackers would set fire to homes. Of course, Montgomery's stubbornness made him dig in and refuse to relocate from his new settlement, especially since he barely afforded to move into that current homestead in the first place. To make matters worse, he was forty years old and instead of being prone to being bullied, he became irritated and resentful. After making his personal and political position known and being civilly outspoken against slavery, he was terrorized, shot at, and forced to secure protection for himself and his family.

In the summer of 1856, George W. Clarke plundered, robbed, and burned out of house and home nearly every free-state settler in Linn County, while his hands were steeped in innocent blood and the light of burning buildings marked his course.[4] That early fall, Montgomery's cabin was attacked and deemed a target, so John Kagi was secured to serve as a hired hand for the family. As it turned out, he was visiting when another attack occurred, so he and Montgomery returned fire and chased the assailants off.

Rumors circulated that George W. Clarke was arming the neighboring Miami Indians and bartering away whiskey and arms in return for them to terrorize anti-slavery sympathizers. That sent many into panicked packing, while some county residents even left their possessions behind.[5] As free-state residents had no representation or protection, Montgomery took responsibility to plead their case to the new governor, John H. Geary. Montgomery went to Lecompton to represent the free-stators' position, but although there was fear of the violence spreading, the governor sat prostate and did not offer a solution. Montgomery decided that while he was already away from home, he would travel to Lawrence, where he thought more capital and support existed. There he received some arms and advice.[6]

Unbeknown to Montgomery, the Border Ruffians were making their way to Linn County with Clarke in the lead. He was accompanied by Colonel Fox and roughly 400 men. Fox broke off a group and headed to join others waiting in Paris, Kansas, 6 miles north of Mound City. From there, they were to make their way back to rejoin with Clarke, burning a path back to Mound City. Once back in Mound City, their final intentions were made known. They converged on the home of Montgomery, shot into it, and burned it to the ground. Kagi answered with gunfire, and he, Montgomery's wife and children narrowly made it out alive to watch the cabin burn to the ground.

With a new zeal, Montgomery bought a pistol and a Sharps rifle and began building a fortified abode that the locals dubbed "Fort Montgomery." Though John Brown was ill with a bout of his reoccurring malarial fever at the time, he funded Montgomery's new home, and George Gill, Tidd, and Stevens did the heavy work of building the fortified replacement. They put thick oak and walnut logs vertically and so tightly that they were impenetrable. They positioned the fortress so that it made a good lookout, especially from the second floor. It had a loft for the family to sleep in and a cellar that later hosted fugitive slaves, guided by none other than Harriet Tubman. In the cellar, they dug a crude tunnel that was later used on more than one occasion for Colonel Montgomery to escape a band in search of him.

Once re-established, Montgomery then went about recruiting other "free-soilers" in Missouri and Kansas, and he evolved into the leader of the local Free State movement and organized the "Self-Protective Company" to combat the "border ruffians" of the "Bleeding Kansas" affair.

It was during this recruitment period that Hazlett and Montgomery crossed paths. It is more speculation than fact as to when the actual meeting took place. Montgomery spoke in simple terms of good versus evil, and it was easy for Hazlett to relate to him. He had definite plans, and he was so convincing that his followers grew to even more convincing numbers. If a recruit asked, "Well, what do you want from me?" or "What can I do?" Montgomery offered a decisive, definitive answer.

According to all accounts, Hazlett quickly proved himself a reliable soldier. He was young, strong, energetic, and even most importantly, coachable. In the winter of '58, Hazlett was an officer under Kagi, Montgomery's right-hand man. Hazlett displayed the utmost coolness and daring on several occasions—among others, repelling with ten men a force of eighty, acting as a pretended U.S. Marshal's posse, retreating successfully over bad ground.[7]

Wattles Wages a Political War But Still Uses Brown for Insurance (Summer 1858)

The Wattles were an anti-slavery family who moved to Kansas specifically to get politically involved to sway the settlers of Kansas to be a free state. Augustus was born in Whitesboro, New York, in 1807, and by the time he was in his mid- to late twenties, attending Lane Theological Seminary in Cincinnati, he emerged as the young and energetic up-and-comer leading the intellectual charge against slavery. Lane had a reputation of having the vital role of being an epicenter of abolitionist thought because of their headmaster, Dr. Lyman Beecher. He was the father of Harriet Beecher Stowe, who was famous for her book *Uncle Tom's Cabin*.

Before graduating, Augustus left Lane to open a school of his own for freed and escaped slaves. Soon after, he elicited the help of Susan Lowe to relocate from New York to Cincinnati to work as a teacher. She was patient and effective, and the two were so dynamic that they raised the money to buy enough land to divvy up into small farms to start a settlement of former slaves. They also built a school for boys, and before Augustus knew it, he was in love with Susan. They married on June 24, 1836.

Augustus's brother John was two years younger and much better looking. Unlike his brother, whose face was aging from stress with a high, wrinkled forehead, thick brows, and eyes marked by crows' feet, John had a strong jawline and a pretty-boy cleft on his chin. Augustus's hair was thinning, but John's was thick and lush. His older brother wore a wiry beard with stray gray hairs shooting in their own direction, but John wore sideburns to highlight his strongest features, his thin lips, sharp jaws, and sculpted chin. He followed his influential brother to Cincinnati and worked at the school for black children and young adults. Later, John became the personal tutor of James C. Ludlow, who was a head of the Ohio Antislavery Society and chief financial backer of the *Philanthropist*, an important abolitionist journal.

As Augustus's involvement in the abolitionist cause grew, he began touring and speaking throughout the country, raising money, meeting prominent people, and writing for newspapers and journals. While Augustus put in time being at the center of the abolitionist movement and intellectualizing the inherent destruction that slavery will cause to the country, his brother moved from failed settlement to settlement searching for the utopian society that was a core concept of the emerging American Transcendentalism movement. He was a conductor on the Underground Railroad and stayed involved in organizing on the ground.

When Augustus moved to Kansas, John and his wife Esther moved to the area, too. Initially, they moved to Douglas County, and the two met an intriguing figure of a man named John Brown. Though they enjoyed living in Douglas, they found that their services were more needed in Linn County. The two began with the planning and design of the town of Moneka that they wanted to establish in Linn County. They worked well together because John had the practical applications of a functional society from those that he saw firsthand dissolve into nothingness, and Augustus took care of the administrative duties. Both men were highly creative and politically well-connected. Both were persuasive and knowledgeable in the way of architecture, education, and leadership. There were pro-slavery raids in Lawrence and Douglas Counties, but those steadfastly held to being Free State counties. Places like Linn County, though, fell into the hands of the proponents of slavery, who had driven Free State settlers out.

That is why the brothers thought it more important to live in Linn County more than Douglas. Douglas had its benefits, but it was too much out of the way to make any real difference in the way of flipping the entire state. Moneka was just north of Sugar Mound, an area known to be a hotbed of tension, violence, and destruction of personal property.

As the region became ground zero in the battle of the divided nation, John Brown visited the area regularly, and on July 9, 1858, the first documented meeting between John Brown and James Montgomery took place at Montgomery's mother-in-law's cabin on Sugar Creek. Montgomery identified proponents and opponents, strongholds, and names of men willing to fight for the cause. By now, Montgomery had already built up a reputation that caught the attention of the Governor, John W. Denver, who called him and his loyal followers a band of "murderers and robbers" earlier that summer on May 16. He was quoted as saying, "If the officers of the law will arrest Montgomery and his men ... we will have no trouble in keeping the peace among our people in this region."[8]

As a result of their meeting, Brown and Montgomery made plans for Brown to move into the area as Shubel Morgan.

Brown had been in the area as early as the spring of 1855. He had a half-sister, Florella, who was married to Reverend Samuel Adair, and the two moved to Osawatomie and served as missionaries, spreading the word of God and abolitionism as part of their religion. Brown also had five sons living in nearby communities. That March, not long after the Adairs moved into the area, Brown visited the couple to bring them a wagon full of Sharps rifles and ammo to disperse and help to keep Kansas a free state.

However, the fight to keep Kansas a free state was slowly shifting to the pro-slavery faction. The Adair cabin became Brown's base and point of contact. The constant back and forth, tit-for-tat violent outbursts had been going on for nearly four years. For example, throughout the spring of 1856, a pro-slavery army went into free-soil Lawrence, Kansas, and ransacked their homes and stole what they wanted, including rations, jewelry, and horses; they also terrified townspeople to make them leave.

The Secret Mission (May 24, 1856)

Brown believed in "an eye for an eye" and Old Testament retribution. He was convinced that God punishes those who disobey his word, and he was appalled by the meekness of his fellow abolitionists, who he knew felt despised slavery as deeply as he did; therefore, he made a statement by retaliating to the present violence. The bloodshed that he caused sent ripples across the entire nation and embedded his savagery into history. Brown and eight men went into pro-slavery Pottawatomie Creek and left a horrifying reminder of Brown's callous maliciousness and fury.

He and his five sons (John Jr., Frederick, Owen, Salmon, and Oliver) and three others (his son-in-law Henry Thompson, James Townsley, and Theodore Weiner) went on what he called a "secret mission." He told them, "Something must be done to show these barbarians that we, too, have rights," and he also explained that the goal wasn't just to kill but to "strike fear in their hearts."[9] He vowed that the slave hounds would be shown no mercy and that they are merely vehicles to deliver God's punishment and vengeance.

The night of May 24, 1856, into the early morning hours of March 25, Brown and the men carried with them short, sturdy broadswords and guns. The medieval weapons were of hard, sharp steel easily wielded with a brass grip that looked scaled down to a pommel that gave comfort and balance. The heavy sabers were donated to Brown from a source in Akron, Ohio.[10] The fuller in the middle of the sword was deep and broad, making the blades a bit lighter when cutting through the air.

They approached the cabin of James Doyle and banged on the door. When Doyle answered, the men burst into the cabin with their pistols drawn, overtaking the shocked and stunned family. Brown ordered the men of the family out of the cabin at gunpoint, as he left the women inside helplessly crying and screaming hysterically. Brown looked like a bizarre horror movie caricature with a filthy old, beat up, sweat-stained straw hat with a long-barreled revolver in his belt. He ordered the three Doyle men—James, William, and Drury—out of the cabin and into the yard, and he commanded them to get on their knees.

He preached to Mrs. Doyle, her daughter, and the youngest son John, who was fourteen. He wanted them to tell the story and the message that he had to the world. He forced James to watch the men hacked to death with the broadswords. Blood spurted, heads split, and arms were dismembered and laying on the ground. Then Brown walked over to James Doyle with his gun drawn and put a bullet through his temple.

There are conflicting retellings of the story. The most undramatic is documented on legendsofamerica.com. It had Brown marching the men by gunpoint to Dutch Henry's tavern to have some sort of symbolic trial with them. As they headed back south across Mosquito Creek, Doyle and the boys tried to escape. Brown shot Doyle at that point, and Brown's boys ran down the Doyle boys and killed them with the swords.

In trancelike dazes, the men walked their way to the next cabin down the road. There Allen Wilkinson lived. Wilkinson was the postmaster in the area. He was first a free-soiler, but he saw a political edge to getting elected to the legislature on a pro-slavery ticket. Adair told Brown that Wilkinson was a "trouble maker" who "caused the free-staters great annoyance by intercepting their newspapers—*The National Era*, *The New York Tribune*, and the like: "He hailed the Alabamians on their arrival ... and was supposed to be privy to their plots and threats."[11] While acting as a lay prosecuting lawyer during the first session of Federal Judge Cato's court in Franklin County at Dutch Henry's tavern, he had a run-in with John Brown, Jr. in which he threatened to "shoot and exterminate" Brown's Pottawatomie Rifle Company.[12]

As they approached the house, dogs started barking. Before the men reached the house, Wilkerson called out, "Who's there!"

"I want you to tell me the way to Dutch Henry's," someone called back.[13] After Wilkerson gave the directions to Dutch Henry's tavern, where he lived in the back, the voice mocked, "Come out and show us."

Wilkinson grimaced and opened the door to exit, but his wife, bedridden with measles, begged him not to go. "It's dark. I'm in my nightwear, and it's too dark for me to find my clothes to get dressed. I could tell you just as well without going outdoors," Wilkinson said.[14]

The men seemed to retreat, and their whisperings could ominously be heard from inside the house. They approached the house. "Are you a northern armist?" a voice hollered.[15]

Wilkerson defiantly answered, "I am." It was understood the answer to mean that Wilkinson was opposed to the Northern of Freesoil party.[16]

Another one of the men said, "You are our prisoner. Do you surrender?"

"Gentlemen," Wilkinson said, "I do." He opened the door with his wife crying and pleading with him.

"Then, open the door."

"Just wait until I make light," he called.

"If you don't open it right now, we'll open it for you."

Despite his wife's pleas, Wilkinson opened the door; four men flooded the room. They seized him and ordered him to hurry up and get dressed. They asked if there were more men in the house and then they commenced to ransack the place. They took two saddles, a rifle, and a powder flask.

"Please," Mrs. Wilkinson said, "please, I am sick and need his help. Please leave him be. I am helpless and can't manage on my own."

Wilkinson said, "Yes, please, at least give me time to find someone to wait on her. I will not run off; you have my word. I will meet with you tomorrow or at your beckoning call."

Brown scanned the room. He looked at Wilkinson's wife and then looked over the children. "You have neighbors?" he asked gruffly.

Mrs. Wilkinson said, "Yes, so I have, but they are not here, and I cannot go for them."

The old man replied, "It matters not."[17] Wilkinson was escorted out of the house.

Mrs. Wilkinson found out about her husband's death the next morning when a neighboring old lady found his gashed and mutilated body while walking her dog. His head was split, his throat slashed open, and his side split. His body was left on the side of the road. He was killed about 150 yards from the house in some dead brush.[18] Louisa Jane Wilkinson's testimony of the account was filed in congressional court:

> The old man, who seemed to be the commander, wore soiled clothes and a straw hat, pulled down over his face. He spoke quick, is a tall, narrow-faced, elderly man. I would recognize him if I could see him.[19]

Yet Brown was gone, apparently hiding out in the wilderness. Before he evaporated into thin air, he had one more stop to make. The third house they visited was James Harris's, who was an employee of the Sherman brothers—Dutch Pete, Dutch Will, and the owner of the tavern where the Cato court was held, Dutch Henry. Brown's bloodthirsty band was in search of the pro-slavery rabble-rouser Henry. The Shermans were known to be drunkards and rumors circulated about them being involved in trafficking Indian women, selling them for prostitution, and sexually assaulting them. The whole expedition was to hold his own court, and Brown was furious when he found that Dutch Henry was out of town that evening.

Dutch Henry was a large brute. He ran a supply store, along with the tavern, and his location was a convenient stop at Mosquito Creek for emigrants crossing east and west. This steady business made him a modicum of success. When Brown and his sons stormed the abode, they rounded up and surveyed the group, looking each one closely in the face. Brown picked two men to be dragged out of the house. His son Frederick, Weiner, and Townsley took the two men a short distance from the cabin, and there, Brown began harassing and interrogating them.

Brown considered his next move. Something did not seem quite right, so he had the boys snatch up the men, throw them back inside, and caught William Sherman. They marched "Dutch Bill" back to the Pottawatomie Creek, put him on his knees, and butchered him, blood and grey matter washing away in the stream. Those that took part washed the blood from the evening's events in the water. In an attempt to claim his innocence, Townsley testified that he did not follow suit because his weapon did not touch human flesh.

The event shocked the region. Brown's marketing plan of fear and terror worked. Killing indiscriminately would have not held the same meaning as his method. Those that knew Brown personally could not believe the savagery on display and the fact that the gentle old man that quoted Bible verses would be the same person that was the ringleader of such brutal barbarity. The quote by Jason Brown on display at a Harpers Ferry exhibit by one of the swords from the massacre said, "The thought that it might be true, that my father and his company could do such a thing was terrible ... the most terrible shock that ever happened to my feelings in my life."

A statement by one of the men involved in the massacre who witnessed the events, James Townsley, said that he disapproved of the slaughter and never admitted to taking part in the killings. He said he asked Brown why they were killing these men, and Brown answered: "It must be done for the protection of the Free-state settlers, that it was better than a score of bad men should die than that one free-state man should be driven out."[20]

Townsley said he went on the expedition because he feared for his own life. He said that when he objected to the notion, Brown brandished his weapon and said to him, "Shut up! You are trying to discourage my boys. Dead men tell no tales."[21]

Though all evidence pointed to Brown as the man responsible for the murders, even if he was not the one who slung the swords that severed the life of the men, his descriptions from those allowed to live from the Harris home, the testimony of the Shermans, and those from Mrs. Wilkinson matched identically. Brown literally got away with murder, but his boys were not so lucky. John, Jr., and Jason (who was evidently not involved with the murders) were savagely beaten to death in retaliation. Frederick was shot through the heart and Brown's Station was burnt to the ground.[22]

Frederick was killed in the Battle of Osawatomie later that summer on August 30, 1856, when a small army of pro-slavery men, led by John W. Reid, swarmed the town of Osawatomie, Kansas. It was in response to the events at Pottawatomie, and Frederick attempted a Leonidas feat of holding off an army of around 300–400 with somewhere around forty men.

The Marais des Cygnes Massacre (May 19, 1858)

Another key figure behind the violence along the border was Charles Hamilton. He was responsible for the retaliation of the massacre and the pro-slavery terrorism in the year that followed. Hamilton moved from Georgia to the area to try and help secure the region as pro-slavery. He was a "Border Ruffian" known to strike fear in the hearts of abolitionists and free-staters, and he was seasoned by multiple skirmishes along the border.

His deep-seated hatred for Montgomery stemmed from an incident in early May when Montgomery besieged Hamilton's fortified home, causing him to leave the territory but resolved to return and take revenge on his former neighbors.[23]

Therefore, on May 19, 1858, Hamilton returned to the Marais des Cygnes River Valley with a twenty-five-man army prepared to pillage, plunder, and murder. They went farm-to-farm, nabbing guys in the fields or in their homes. They took every male that they came into contact with, and they took what they wanted from their homes and farms.

When they got to the home of a blacksmith named Eli Snyder, he refused to go peacefully and began firing at the men as they approached. They returned fire, and a bullet bit through a part of his leg. He abandoned his farm and ran back into the woods and escaped.

The armed band forged ahead, rounding up a large group of men. They weeded out the old, the young, and other Freemasons, and then they made the remaining eleven men put their hands behind their heads and marched them to a ravine and made them kneel. William Stilwell of Sugar Mound was one of them. "Sirs," he pleaded, "I am known in this area as one who doesn't take a side. I have a beautiful wife and two small children. I am here from Indiana only to stake a claim for myself. I have never taken part in any of the violence anywhere. I am a peaceful man and, I, too, am a Freemason."

"Not taking sides is as harmful as being a Jayhawk," said a Dr. Hamilton from Fort Scott. "You want to take my rights away? I'll take your life away."

"I want you to have your rights."

"What have you done to protect our states' rights?"

"I am a peaceful man. I have done nothing, sir."

"Exactly! You are either for me or against me," sneered Dr. Hamilton. He raised his double-barreled shotgun, loaded with pistol balls.[24]

"Please," sobbed Stilwell, "don't allow my children to grow up without a father. I have nothing to do with any of this."

Hamilton told the executioners to raise their guns and wait for his command to fire, and then Charles Hamilton gave the order, "Fire!" There was a rain of gunshots.

Dr. Hamilton, a Freemason, squeezed the trigger of his shotgun, the charge entering Stilwell's left breast.[25] The firing squad rummaged through the dead bodies, taking what they wanted, and putting some extra slugs into those that showed signs of life.

Hamilton and his men escaped back into Missouri. Eventually, Hamilton moved back to Georgia, and later, he was commissioned as an officer for the Confederacy in the Civil War. Along with Stilwell, four others laid dead. Five were wounded, and one went unharmed. A Baptist clergyman named Charles Reed, who had only moved into the area from Wisconsin about a week ago, was shot, but he faked his death and crawled off into the bushes to escape.[26] His wife searched all night for "Preacher Reed," as he was called, and she found him the next morning near death. She had the men taken back into the town of Trading Post, where the dead were properly addressed, and the wounded cared for.

William Tomlinson wrote about the incident and entering the "house of death" where the mangled corpses were clearly exposed to view.

> All had received the fire in the front. Not a scar disfigured the back of one of the ultimately dead, but Oh, where once beat the gallant hearts, thick, thick as the drops of a summer shower had dashed the leaden hail of death ... On the cold, pallid lips of the martyred Stilwell there rested a faint smile, as though of wife and Heaven were his last thoughts on earth.[26]

Hazlett Meets John Brown (Fall 1858)

Albert joined up with James Montgomery while he and his brother were making ends meet to maintain the farm in Prescott. Robbing and stealing from pro-slavery farms had its rewards. To supplement his meager income, Albert resold or traded horses or goods that he had acquired through raids and looting.

One afternoon, James Montgomery made a visit to his brother's farm. "I have a friend," he said to Albert, "who I think, you'd like to meet him. He is in search of a fine stallion, just like the one you brought back from Missouri. He has a land warrant in which you might be interested."

"Well, when can I meet this friend of yours?"

"He is due into town tonight. We can meet him at our mutual friend's house, Augustus Wattles. Wattles wrote and summoned him for help. When you meet the old man, he will be introduced as Shubel Morgan."

"The deal must be a good one," replied Hazlett. "A stallion of this pedigree won't come easy."

"Money or material possessions are of no consequence to this man," laughed Montgomery. "This man is connected to wealthy abolitionists, and he has control of their purse strings. I can guarantee a lucrative trade."

That fall evening in 1858, John Brown returned to Kansas for the first time since the murders that the newspapers dubbed the "Pottawatomie Creek Massacre." Brown said that he wanted to reestablish roots there because of the importance of the area in the fight. Brown was late, but one of the men had a jug of bourbon that they shared by taking a hit, wincing, and then passing it along to the next. After Brown arrived, he met all of the men and quickly conducted business with each one on a personal basis, even though it was apparent that he had met none of them before. Hazlett respected his no-nonsense demeanor and was instantly drawn to the old man, who spoke eloquently and passionately about wreaking violence and mayhem. While he spoke, his eyes quickly scanned the next man in line, assessing his potential as a soldier.

He approached Albert and said, "About this stallion that James is telling me about, whattaya want for him?"

"A substantial sum of money," Hazlett responded.

"You mean to tell me you don't have an exact figure that you were thinking about asking for him?"

"No, I was kinda hoping that you had an idea of how much you'd want to pay for him."

"How about land?" Brown asked. "Have you considered a swap? Would you take land for the stallion? Land will last you a lifetime. Money ... eh ... money fades. You'll spend the money. You will always have the land. America prints money every day, but God's not making any more land."

"How much land are we talking about? Whattaya talking here?"

Brown reached down in the breast pocket of his threadbare and dusty overcoat. "What I have here is a United States land warrant for 40 acres. 40 acres not too far from here."

"Well, I think we have a deal, Mister ... err ... Mr ..."

"Morgan. Shubel Morgan."

"Right, right," said Hazlett. "We have a deal, Mr. Morgan," he said smiling and extending his hand.

Brown shook on the deal. "And your name? I'm not sure I got your name."

Albert thought for a moment. "William Harrison," he confidently said.

Brown instantly saw an opportunity in Hazlett and another young man who was at this meeting. Both had come highly recommended by Montgomery. The evening ended with Brown acquiring two new energetic recruits—Hazlett and a twenty-six-year-old by the name of Jeremiah "Jerry" Goldsmith Anderson. Anderson was from Iowa, and he was thin with dark hair. His quiet demeanor collided with the reputation of the brutal violence that followed him. Brown told his new talent that he was leaving town, but this house, Wattles' home, was home base and that he would be in touch with the two men later in a few months.

"The Parallels" (December 20, 1858–June 1859)

Brown summoned Hazlett and Jerry Anderson back to Wattles' home. Spending months on the road, Brown was traveling and fundraising and not paying attention to political nuances that were taking place, but it was clear that slavery was losing at the polling booth in Kansas; however, that April, Congress passed a pro-slavery English Bill, trying to suppress the violence by federally mandating Kansas a slave state. When the English Bill came up for a vote in Kansas on August 2, it was defeated by a staggering 10.5:1 margin.[28]

Then, Governor Denver resigned, and Hugh Walsh became the acting governor. Walsh was from Alabama and was known to help the Border Ruffians in controlling the territory and keeping Montgomery and his men at bay. Walsh was turning back the clock and putting more power into the hands of pro-slavery groups until Wattles, who knew about the events on the ground as well as being dialed into those political maneuvers that indicate power losses, wrote Brown asking for his style of influence.

Walsh set a $500 reward for Brown and $300 for Montgomery. Captain A. J. Weaver went to arrest the two men, but Brown was out of town, and Montgomery, along with Hazlett and other men, fought the brigade of deputized marshals off after being tipped off that they were coming.

To make a statement and a counterattack, Montgomery focused his attention on Fort Scott. The sheriff held fellow abolitionist Benjamin Rice at the Fort Scott Hotel, a business that Montgomery, Hazlett, and others unsuccessfully tried to burn down in June. They stacked hay and tinder along the hotel, but before it really caught, they were found out and driven off with a bombardment of gunshots. Now, on December 14, Brown came to town to assist Montgomery and his men in the liberation of a free-state man. Montgomery took the lead in the planning and execution of the ploy, while Brown resigned himself to take a more supporting role. When the news broke that the hotel was blitzed and Rice was broken out of confinement, Brown was to blame.

Rice was arrested on a murder charge, but Montgomery asserted that he was being jailed in the hotel illegally. Some say that the men on duty that night were in on the raid, and the mission was to be "bloodless." When the outfit burst through the door, the guards were easily taken, and their weapons were said to be preassembled in a pile on the floor.

Deputy Marshal John Little was keeping the sutlers' store a short way down and across the street. He peered out the store window, noticing Rice surrounded and the guards being forced down the street at gunpoint. He watched the procession of men approaching the store and had an opportunity to ambush them. As the contingent passed by his store, Little opened the door and fired at short range into the crowd with No. 2 buckshot, wounding Ben Seaman and John Kagi. After the shot, Little went to a side door and looked out through a transom; being noticed by a member of the posse, he received a bullet from a Sharps rifle and was instantly killed.[29]

Hazlett and another man were ordered into the store to take all that was of value. They went into the store, stepped over Little's body, gathered what could be pocketed and easily carried, ran out the back door, and caught back up to the group down the street.

Even though things had not gone as planned with Little's death, Montgomery considered the mission a success. To Brown, on the other hand, it did not have the meaningful discharge that he was hoping for. On the brighter side, though, he found a proven, dutiful legionnaire in Albert Hazlett.

Brown admired Hazlett as a warrior. He was steady and never flinched at gunshots, ready at an instance to expect the unexpected. He stayed calm and gave clear, direct orders when taking control of hostages or a situation. His demeanor jumped him up in the ranks, and though he had already won the favor of Montgomery from past events, he was now considered one of Brown's mercenary men. Hazlett's loyalty to both leaders never wavered, yet he knew that to make more of an impact on the direction of the country and in the long run make every state a free state, it was John Brown who would prove to be more influential.

Brown was receiving pressure from his financial supporters to do something to appeal to the more humane and just to strike at the heart of slavery. His riotous stunts were sending the wrong message. The perfect opportunity presented itself a few days after the Fort Scott rescue mission. One of his men, George Gill, brought to him a light-skinned slave from Missouri who he encountered while on patrol along the border.

"Captain," started Gill, "as I was scouting down the line, I ran across this colored man, whose ostensible purpose was the selling of brooms."[30]

"What is your name, sir?" Brown asked.

"Theys call me Jim, sah, Jim Daniels," the man answered.

"George here says that you're in quite a predicament," said Brown.

"Yessah, my fambly is about to be sep'rated and sold," Jim said, holding back tears. "My massa said that my two babe boys is the perfect age for market. My wife will be sol' for spite. Theys gonna be sol' at an admin'strators' sale in the 'mediate future. But it's not just me and my family, sah, theys others that'll lose they fambly."

Oddly elated, Brown determined that here was an opportunity to carry an attack against slavery itself.[31] "God has sent you to me," he said to Daniels. "God has provided me a basis of action.[31] I promise you, sir, we will take immediate action against those that threaten you. We will strike tomorrow as we intend to keep you and all the other families in your area intact."

Brown planned to take two groups of crusaders and cut two paths to gather a group of slaves and rejoin on the other side of the mission to return to Kansas. From Kansas, they intended to make their way north to Canada. In one group, Brown and ten others were to take over Harvey Hicklan's estate, where Jim and his family lived. The other party—made up of Aaron Stevens, Hazlett, Tidd, and about five others—were to go on a somewhat parallel path to gather slaves of their own. Quickness, the element of surprise, and stealth were the cornerstones of the mission to prevent the men from pillaging and plundering to avoid unnecessary bloodshed.

With this standard, the plan was a failure, for when the Hicklan estate was overtaken, the men took advantage of the situation and stole what they wanted. In Hazlett's group, an innocent man was shot and killed.

Around midnight on the 20th, the men stole into Missouri. Brown wanted the act to serve as a symbolic gesture and a rejection of slavery as an ideal, but the character of the men in his charge was in question. With Brown was a notorious horse thief nicknamed "Pickles," Jerry Anderson, Gill, Kagi and others. Gill oversaw the marauders and was in charge of keeping the integrity of the mission by ethically taking sole property of slaves. Of this task, Gill said, "I soon discovered that watches and other articles were being taken; some of our number proved to be more adventurers, ready to take from friend or foe as opportunity offered."[33]

Five slaves were gathered up and taken from the "Lawrence Estate," of which Hicklan was the master and administrator. Besides the fugitive slaves, there was a long list of other stolen items, including horses, oxen, a wagon, food supplies, shotguns, coats and clothes, jugs of whiskey, and other items.

From there, they ventured a quarter of a mile to the John Larue estate and found five more slaves willing to risk life and limb to escape to freedom. The men then went on to ravage the Larue estate, taking similar items that they accrued from the Lawrence estate.

Under Stevens, Hazlett and the others were to take over the holdings of David Cruise and Hugh Martin. At the Cruise house, they were to retrieve a fourteen-year-old girl that the Daniels family specifically requested.

There is a yarn woven about Cruise accidentally shooting himself, for when the men came banging the door yelling and cursing, he jumped out of bed with his revolver. He fired on the men, but since the cylinder was entangled in a ribbon from the bedclothes, the gun misfired. When he threw the gun down on the floor in frustration and fear, it discharged, "and the old man fell near the fireplace and died almost instantly, his blood flowing out upon the hearth-stone."[34]

Another account by Cruise's young son, Rufus, marks Hazlett as the killer. In a letter he wrote later in 1887, he said the men gained entry and trust by pretending to be travelers in search of a night's shelter. Cruise called off the dogs and agreed to feed and provide shelter for the night. Sitting around the fire, one of the men pulled his revolver on Cruise. Rufus wrote that it was "Al Hazlitt [*sic.*]" who drew the pistol. "I broke out of the house on the porch, and I heard the pistol shot that killed father. I am sure it was Al Hazlitt shot him." Barefoot and in his nightclothes, Rufus fled 3 miles over snow-covered ground to the house of Mr. Mitchell, a relative.[35]

Another rendition, maybe more closely to the truth, plays out differently. David Cruise was rumored to have at his house some gold buried on the premises, which even though Brown's mission was to take possession of slaves as property and forego inanimate property, a little gold would be helpful. Cruise was a hard-working farmer, who was not rich by any stretch but had more than most, even owning two slaves. He was an old German, who spoke limited English, so when Stevens gained entry to the house and demanded the girl, Cruise either truly misunderstood Stevens or pretended to misunderstand his instructions to get the slave girl. Cruise motioned for Stevens to follow him.

Leaving the men standing around the fire of the main room, Stevens went to go to where Cruise was encouraging him to go when Cruise grabbed his revolver and pulled it on Stevens. In the confusion, Rufus bolted from the house, and the other men seized Mrs. Cruise and put a gun to her head. Forever claiming self-defense, Stevens shot Cruise through the chest.[36] The old man's eyes lit up, he grabbed at his chest, and then collapsed dead before he hit the floor. A pool of blood instantly gathering around the stone-hearth.

The men snatched up the crying woman and forced her to lead them through the house, opening closets, drawers, and cupboards. They stole from the ranch. One of the men rummaged through Cruise's pants that sat by his bed on a chair, and there they found $30 in gold.[38] Hints of the rumored buried gold of which they never found.

They went outside and took what they wanted from the farm, horses, a wagon filled with provisions, two oxen, jewelry, and the female slave that they were sent for; her name was Jane, and she was in the very last stages of her pregnancy.

In the letter, Rufus also said that Jane saw the men coming and started to laugh. "She went back into the kitchen," he wrote, "and began to pack up. She took with her $60 in money, part hers and part my mother's."[38]

As for the other slave at the estate, his name was George. Rufus said that George "was away from home sparking a slave woman at the nearby Martin home," but historian Patrick Brophy asserts that George was home but fled in terror, hiding from his would-be liberators, choosing to faithfully stay with his murdered master's family.[39]

Several indications corroborate the fact that Stevens killed Cruise, despite what Rufus and George Gill later wrote to create the historical controversy that followed. The most damning evidence is Stevens' very own confession. Those who stayed at the farmhouse before the Harpers Ferry raid later recounted the story that Stevens told one night out of guilt and boredom. Stevens said that he "thoughtlessly" followed Cruise when the old man "slipped behind him and pulled a gun."[40] He said that it then became a "case of shoot first. You might call it a case of self-defense, or you might say that I had no business in there and the old man was right."[41]

Then later, when Stevens was mortally wounded and thought to be dying, he admitted to firing the shot that killed Cruise. Lastly, years after the event, Jane, the freed slave girl, said that she saw Stevens shoot her former master with her own eyes.

When the two bands met up again that night, the first thing that Brown recognized was that Hazlett was riding a new horse. They went to the Fort Bayne area and camped out in the snow and cold. Down in the deep ravine to dodge some of the wind and muffle as much of their noise as they could, they camped all day. They had a few rations to eat and share with one another but not nearly enough for the size of the party. They could not dare risk detection by starting a fire. When night began to fall again, they trekked the 10 miles back to headquarters, Augustus Wattles' home. When they arrived in the middle of the night, Mrs. Wattles began fixing them something to eat, knowing that they would be famished.

Montgomery and some of the other men were there waiting for Brown's return. "How is it captain?" Montgomery said in greeting. "Whom have you here?"[42]

Brown's face was beet red and wind burnt. He smiled and poked out his chest. "Allow me to introduce you to a part of my family," he said. "Observe, I have carried the war into Africa."[43] With dramatic flair, he waved his hat over the first group of slaves that he had assembled.

All sat, ate, and talked. It continued to be a joyous affair until Stevens begrudgingly had to report the dower news of the death of David Cruise. The room went silent and grew darker. Brown, Montgomery, and Wattles made eye contact with one another, and without saying a word, they got up, went into the other room, and closed the door.

Brown went to the desk and sat down. Montgomery and Wattles were distraught that Brown had violated the political pact that the two viewed as paving the pathway for Kansas to become a free state, "The Sugar Mound Peace Agreement." Montgomery and Wattles viewed the first step in eliminating slavery in America was to make Kansas a free state.

"John," Wattles pleaded, "this will hurt our cause. The tables were turning in our direction, and now this? Lawless raiding and murdering. America will not stand for it. We will be viewed as the savages, instead of those who believe in bondage and torture as a means for economic gain."

"He is right, John," started Montgomery, "you know that I will not back down to violence, but that way was not working. Without a civil war, we cannot go farm to farm and kill our fellow Americans."

Brown began scratching out something on a piece of paper that Wattles had on the desk. He listened quietly as Wattles and Montgomery went on chastising the carelessness of his and his men's actions.

Finally, he spoke. "I have considered the matter well; you will have no more attacks from Missouri; I shall now leave Kansas, probably you will never see me again. I consider it my duty to draw the scene of the excitement to some other part of the country."[44] Brown went to work on writing what is now known as "The Parallels," justification for this Missouri raid. In presenting it to Wattles and Montgomery, he said, "Gentlemen, I would like to have your attention for a few minutes. I usually leave the newspaper work to Kagi, but this time I have something to say myself.[45]

Brown's men—including Hazlett, the male slaves, and two white hostages—slept under the wagons that night, and the slave women and children were taken to Augustus's brother John's house.

It did not take long for the news of the murder of the admired old man to get around and spark outrage in the county and eventually across the country. Brown knew he had to lay low and hide the eleven freed slaves, so he took them into Franklin County. There they stayed about a month, but a few days after their arrival, the number of fugitives was increased by one with the birth of Jane's baby.

When Brown felt safe to move on toward freedom in Canada, the excursion began north. Hazlett assisted as a chaperone. When they neared Holton on January 31, they were ambushed by pro-slavery men hoping to earn the bounty money placed on Brown's head and the fugitive slaves. These men were from Atchison. Brown, Hazlett, and the others never retreated. Brown's reputation and fierce determination were so threatening to the forty-five or so U.S. marshals that they retreated without a single shot fired. To mock the event, the stare-down became known as "The Battle of the Spurs," referring to the horseback retreat of pro-slavery forces.

Three months and 11,000 miles later, the escorts traveled their precious cargo through Kansas, Iowa, Illinois, and Michigan. Brown, with the help of loyal soldiers like Hazlett, made his way to Canada and freedom on March 12, 1859. Returning to the Cleveland area (where it can be speculated that Hazlett had friends from his earlier day living there), Hazlett and Brown separated.

Hazlett eventually went back to Kansas, where he spent time with his brother preparing the farm and early spring planting. Before leaving Brown, he was put on watch. Brown told him that he was proud of his service to him, and their impact would be even greater on the country. He was planning something that would bring the institution of slavery to its knees, and since he was such an important cog in the wheel, he would be called upon again for his help.

Montgomery and Wattles worked more politically on the institution, but those wheels ground too slowly for the likes of Brown and Hazlett.

Wattles concentrated on establishing Moneka as a town, and his brother John joined in that endeavor. In fact, his brother started a school, and soon after establishing an academy in a large building that he designed, he lobbied Congress to get the funding to build a railroad connecting Emporia, Kansas, to Jefferson City, Missouri. Soon after, John died suddenly on September 20, 1959.

While on watch, Hazlett spent time going back and forth between working with his brothers in Kansas and going back to the homestead in Indiana. While back in Indiana, he became bored with the mundane farm life, and on May 21, 1859, he wrote to John Brown. He said, "I wish it would come off soon, for I am tired of doing nothing."[46]

Hazlett was working on his neighbor's farm when he received a letter that had instructed him to meet John Brown at a boarding house in Chambersburg, Pennsylvania. That letter changed his life.

APPENDIX

Timeline of Events

The goals of this final analysis are to give more than a simplistic timeline of events, to offer explanations to patch up any holes that may have occurred from the creative nonfiction narrative, to give tidbits left out for the sake of clarity and tightness, and to present justification and in some cases explanations for the choices used in the text.

September 21, 1837—Absalom "Albert" Hazlett was born. He was the sixth child of Alexander and Sarah Hazlett. Some accounts have his name listed as Absalom C. Hazlett and others have Absalom G. Hazlett. No initial is used on the 1850 census form.

November 7, 1837—John Brown stood up in Elijah Lovejoy's funeral and vowed to end slavery. Brown referred back to this day often throughout the course of his life.

1850—The census has Absalom listed at twelve years old. It was around this time that Alexander was said to have inherited 50 acres from his sister Mary McKane and settled into Green Township. Before that, Alexander was a stonemason moving from area to area to maintain steady work. Green Township farms were livestock farms focused on cattle, sheep, and the production of wool. According to the census, the main crops in the area were buckwheat, wheat, rye, corn, and oats. Green Township led the county in butter and cheese production.

The Developmental Teenage Years—Certain local stories mark Hazlett's teenage years as a troubled youth, seeking attention that he never received, even from his mother who never sent word or acknowledged him during his time in prison. He was said to have been a horse thief in New York. Also, he worked as a boatman on the Pennsylvania Canal in Johnstown under John McGovern when he took a trip over the mountains, disposed of the boat and team, and pocketed the money. When caught, he returned the money to avoid prosecution. He spent time in Ohio and was believed to have joined up with a band of Free State men who ventured to the Kansas border to cause trouble. When he returned to Indiana County for work, he was hired by John B. Allison, and he bragged about being grazed by a bullet.

There is a story worth noting here that was left out of the narrative from this time period with Allison. It comes from the writings of Clarence Stephenson in the *Indiana Gazette's* Bicentennial Edition. While harvesting oats for Allison, Hazlett had the letter B carved into his blade. He asked Allison if he knew what it stood for, and of course Allison didn't. Hazlett said it stood for "Blood, and all the oats bore the same impression, and the time is near at hand when it was to be shed." Allison pushed further, and Hazlett continued, "Blood was to be spilt in liberation of the slave." He told Allison that he was connected with a company who "were pledged to the overthrow of slavery." Allison paid him no mind and took it as ramblings of an over-imaginative teen but later recounted the story after Hazlett was tried and hanged.

1854—The Kansas–Nebraska Act puts the decision of whether or not to allow slavery in the new territories into the hands of the people in those states. This act triggered an unfortunate series of events. James Montgomery moved to Jackson County in Missouri and then later to Linn County, Kansas. There, he organized Free State settlers and led what he called the "Self-Protective Company."

October 7, 1855—Hatred brewing and anarchy on the rise, border ruffians from Missouri commit voter fraud and organize a bogus legislature in Shawnee Mission enacting draconian pro-slavery laws. In opposition, a Free State constitution is presented in Topeka and ratified by anti-slavery settlers.

May 1856—Albert's father, Alexander, died. The exact date is impossible to confirm; however, newspaper clues and letters can be used to support this month and year. Apparently, the family was not respected, and the boys had a reputation of being shady ruffians, so not much attention was paid to Alexander's death.

May 25, 1856—The Pottawatomie Creek Massacre occurred, where five pro-slavery men were murdered under the direction of John Brown.

September 1856—Brown earns the name of "Osawatomie Brown" after his badly outnumbered men won a battle against proslavery forces at Osawatomie, Kansas. It was rumored that Hazlett took part in this battle, but nothing can be used to corroborate the rumor. Also, it does not coincide with what we substantially know to be the first meeting between Hazlett and Brown. If he took part, he was not directly under Brown.

Early 1857—Hazlett arrived in Kansas. Some Indiana residents claimed it was by way of Ohio, and others say it happened as outlined in the narrative. It was John Brown who wrote in his diary that Hazlett made his escape to Kansas after being charged with larceny of overcoats.

December 1857—It was about this time that James Montgomery was recruiting men to push pro-slavery settlers out of Bourbon County, where Hazlett was staying with his brother John in Prescott, Kansas. It is believed to be at this point when Hazlett joined forces with Montgomery. Skirmishes began giving the Free State men the upper hand.

May 19, 1858—Pro-slavery men marched ten Free State men to a ravine and opened fire on them. They killed five and wounded the five others in what is known as "The Marais des Cygnes Massacre."

July 9, 1858—John Brown and James Montgomery meet and join forces.

Fall 1858—Montgomery introduces Hazlett to John Brown. The exact date is unknown, but the circumstances were made clear with several documented retellings all in line with each other.

December 16, 1858—Hazlett assisted James Montgomery in freeing Ben Rice from being held at the Western Hotel in Fort Scott.

December 19, 1858—Hazlett aided John Brown in freeing 11 slaves and escorting them to Detroit, where they crossed into Windsor, Canada to their freedom. Hazlett was charged with the murder of David Cruise but never arrested. The event covered 82 days and over 1,000 miles.

May 21, 1859—Hazlett writes John Brown telling him, "I wish it would come off soon, for I am tired of doing nothing."

July 3, 1859—John Brown signs the lease for Kennedy Farm under the name of "Isaac Smith."

August 16, 1859—John Brown and Frederick Douglass have the infamous meeting in Chambersburg.

July–September 1859—No clear date is given for when Hazlett arrived at Kennedy Farm. Almost immediately after signing the lease and setting up the old farmhouse, Brown began recruiting and getting the word out to his men. Some say Hazlett arrived soon after, and given his ambition, this makes sense and is aligned with his character. Others say that it was not until September for when he arrived. If this is the case, there are indications that he spent some time in Chambersburg with Kagi, so perhaps, instead of reporting straight to the farmhouse, he went to the Ritner House and then to the Kennedy Farm. This would make sense, given his reliance upon Mrs. Cook for help at the Ritner House. For the sake of story and character, Hazlett was with the first group of men to arrive at the Farmhouse.

October 16, 1859—Brown leads his men into Harpers Ferry.

October 17, 1859—Local citizens fight back, pinning down Brown and seizing the bridge.

October 18, 1859—U.S. Marines arrive, capture Brown, and restore order. Hazlett and Anderson flee.

October 21, 1859—Clarence Stephenson asserts in his July 3, 1976, article for the *Indiana Gazette Bicentennial Celebration* that the pistol was traded to a man named Charles Brewster in Oakville, Pennsylvania. He said that Brewster "was a man of great selfishness and often regretted that he did not detain Hazlett for reward. He did not suspect who he was at the time." However, this narrative uses the Kansas Historical Society rendition. The K.H.S. has the actual pistol in their collection and has its lineage starting with Robert Smith, who was given the revolver for a night's stay at the hotel.

October 22, 1859—Hazlett is brought to justice by Bill Houser and Charlie Campbell. As stated in the text, there are various retellings of the arrest of Hazlett, but this version presented is based on the research of Joseph D. Cress. Cress is an education/history reporter for *The Sentinel* in Carlisle, Pennsylvania. He is the authority of the history of that region. Cress's story is based on the writings of W. J. Shearer, Hazlett's self-appointed attorney.

When arrested, Hazlett used the name William Harrison, which may or may not have been the first use of this alias, but he maintained this moniker until his death. Confidant and author Richard J. Hinton said that he was "sympathetically drawn more closely to this young man than any other of the John Brown party" because he used the name that Hinton created and used for "prudential reasons" in signing letters to Kagi. Learning the art of using a fake identity early, Hazlett undoubtably used various names, but for continuity purposes, William Harrison is used throughout the manuscript.

October 29, 1859—Hazlett appeared before a judge in Carlisle on a writ of *habeas corpus*, but he failed to convince the judge that he was being unfairly held because of mistaken identity.

November 2, 1859—After a week of trial and forty-five minutes of deliberation in Virginia, John Brown is found guilty of murder, treason, and inciting a slave insurrection.

November 5, 1859—Hazlett is extradited to Charlestown to stand trial for murder, treason, and inciting a slave insurrection.

December 2, 1859—John Brown is hanged. Jailer John Avis wrote that the only thing Brown said on the gallows to him was, "Be quick."

February 13, 1860—Hazlett and Stevens were sentenced to be hanged.

March 1, 1860—Hazlett writes Anne Brown, accepting his fate.

March 15, 1860—Hazlett writes Rebecca Spring to ask her to take his body "from this land of chains." In the letter, is his memorable quote, "I am willing to die in this cause of liberty; if I had ten thousand lives, I would willingly lay them all down for the same cause."

March 16, 1860—Hazlett and Stevens are hanged.

March 19, 1860—Hazlett and Stevens are buried in Perth Amboy, New Jersey.

August 30, 1899—A funeral was organized to gather all the raiders together to be buried at the John Brown Farm Cemetery at North Elba, Essex County, New York.

Endnotes

Chapter 1

1 Clarence Stephenson was not at the ceremony, but I am sure that he would have liked to have been there. He was heavily involved up to the point when his age made it impossible for him to take part in events. Everyone in town knew him or knew of him and his contributions to the history of the county. I have spoken with him on numerous occasions and spent time with him in a public setting, book signings, commemorative events, etc. I talked to him over the phone several times in reference to the writing of my book, *Pennsylvania's Coal and Iron Police*. In 1964, he wrote a book entitled *The Impact of the Slavery Issue on Indiana County*. Given that book and my discussions with him, I could imagine the type of speech that he would give during this marker unveiling, and that is the basis for his speech that he never really gave in this chapter. Clarence Stephenson, 92, died on August 13, 2011, so in a sense this is an homage to Mr. Stephenson.

2 Historical and Genealogical Society of Indiana County, "John Brown's Army: The Man From Indiana County" (Retrieved from google.com/amp/s/hgsic.wordpress.com/2020/02/11/john-browns-army-the-man-from-indiana-county/amp/).

3 *Ibid.*

4 *Ibid.*

Chapter 2

1 Louis A. DeCaro, Jr., an associate professor at Alliance Theology Seminary in New York City, is a leading authority on John Brown. He is an editor and author of a host of books, scholarly articles, and journals. He curates a website in which he posted this article: Wolfe, H. S., "The Second Harpers Ferry Raid: The Fate of John Brown's Men," *John Brown the Abolitionist—A Biographer's Blog*, (Retrieved from abolitionist-john-brown.blogspot.com/2015/09/the-second-harpers-ferry-raid-fate-of.html

2 *Ibid.*

3 *Ibid.*

4 *Ibid.*

5 *Ibid.*

6 *Ibid.*
7 Featherstonhaugh, T., "The Final Burial of the Followers of John Brown," *The New England Magazine*, vol. 24, pp. 128–134. (Boston: Warren F. Kellogg, 1901).
8 Nasby, D., *Harpers Ferry: Images of America, West Virginia* (Charleston, SC: Arcadia Publishing, 2004), p. 28.
9 Feathersonhaugh, T., *op. cit.*, p. 132.
10 *Ibid.*
11 Nasby, D., *op. cit.*, p. 29.
12 Feathersonhaugh, T., *op. cit.*, p. 133
13 Barry, J., *The Strange Story of Harpers Ferry: With Legends of the Surrounding Country*, (Martinsburg, WV: Thompson Brothers, 1903), p. 95.
14 The article "The Conspirator's Biographies" is a compilation of two different sources: Connelley, W. E., *John Brown*, (Topeka: Crane & Company, 1900), 340–347; and Villard, O., *John Brown 1800–1859: A Biography Fifty Years After* (1910, reprint, Gloucester, MA: Peter Smith, 1965), 678–687. It is credited to ASR-3/21/1995: Retrieved from www2.iath.virginia.edu/jbrown/men.html.
15 Nasby, D., *op. cit.*, p. 28.
16 Featherstonhaugh, T., *op. cit.*, p. 133.
17 Wolfe, S., *op. cit.*, 2015.
18 No transcript of Bishop Potter's speech can be found today; however, his writings and beliefs can be researched and read. The speech in the text is patterned and quoted from the passage from the book *All Things Human*. Bourgeois, M., *All Things Human: Henry Codman Potter and the Social Gospel in the Episcopal Church* (Urbana & Chicago: University of Illinois Press, 2004), p. 64.
19 Whitelaw Reid's speech was taken from an actual speech that he gave at an editor's conference. The transcript was published in *The Goodland News* in Kansas. "Whitelaw Reid on the Independent Press," *The Goodland Republic and Goodland News*, vol. 8, p. 4 (Goodland, Kansas: J.H. Stewart, 1899).
20 This prayer and speech was created and quoted from a biography of Joshua Young written by Malinda Green and Karen G. Johnston found on *The Dictionary of Unitarian and Universalist Biography* web page, which is curated and copyrighted by the Unitarian Universalist History and Heritage Society (UUHHS). Green, M., and Johnson, K. G., "Joshua Young," *The Dictionary of Unitarian and Universalist Biography,* Groton, MA, 2018). Retrieved from uudb.org/articles/joshuayoung.html
21 *Ibid.*
22 *Ibid.*

Chapter 3

1 Stephenson, C., "A Harpers Ferry Insurectionist [*sic.*]," *The Indiana Evening Gazette,* July 3, 1976, Bicentennial Edition, pp. f–22.
2 *Ibid.*
3 *Ibid.*
4 *Ibid.*
5 *Ibid.*
6 *Ibid.*
7 *Ibid.*
8 *Ibid.*
9 *Ibid.*
10 Cress, J. D., "Cumberland County's Connection to John Brown's Raid at Harpers Ferry," *Cumberland County History*, vol. 26, pp. 48–60 (57), (Carlisle, PA: The

Cumberland County Historical Society, 2009).

11 *Ibid.*

12 This quote is from the article, "More about the Hazlett Family" that ran in an old weekly newspaper, *The Indiana Messenger*, on June 30, 1897. The article documents the story of the attempted jail break with Jonas trading places with his brother. This story cannot be corroborated with research. The credibility of the story is in question, for there were other errors in the story, like misnaming his cell mate as "Stephenson" instead of "Stevens." It also asserts that Hazlett and "Stephenson" were arrested together by a man giving them a ride into town soon after they crossed the Pennsylvania state line. It read, "No sooner were they seated in the carriage than the stranger drew a revolver on them and made them his prisoners." This contradicts all other stories of the two separate arrests. True, Hazlett's arrest is somewhat clouded by some retellings and lack of finite details, but Stevens' arrest is well documented that Stevens was wounded and captured by the militia in "John Brown's Fort." Another major discrepancy in the article is that it states, "Miss Stephenson, his intended bride, took his corpse along with her brother's to Eaglewood Cemetery, Perth Amboy, New Jersey." There are no author credits insinuating it was written by editorial staff, but it was said, "Our inquiries in regard to Hazlett" had brought new information about Hazlett's significance to the area. As for the information it detailed, "The article appended is furnished by a young lady friend of White township, who gathered the facts from her father's lips several years ago." "More about the Hazlett Family," *The Indiana Messenger*, (Indiana, PA: S.A. Smith &Bro., 1897), vol. 42, no. 22, p. 3.

13 Hinton, R., *John Brown and His Men* (New York: Funk and Wagnalls Company, 1894), pp. 526–527.

14 The excerpts from the correspondence between Hazlett and Rebecca Spring come from her memoirs. The original manuscript with her own handwritten revisions are housed in Stanford University's Special Collections. Stanford University Department of Special Collections, M0541, Rebecca Spring Papers, box X, folder Y.

15 Stephenson, *op. cit.*

16 Spring, *op. cit.*, p. 156.

17 Spring, *op. cit.*, p. 157.

18 *Ibid.*

19 Stephenson, *op. cit.*, p. f–23.

20 Hinton, R., *op. cit.*, p. 501.

21 Wolfe, S., "The Second Harpers Ferry Raid: The Fate of John Brown's Men."

22 Featherstonhaugh, T., "The Final Burial of the Followers of John Brown," *The New England Magazine*, vol. 24, p. 133.

23 The roundup was accessed through the Newpapers.com archive. The full page of *The Daily News* appears without publishing credits and can be found dated March 30, 1894, at newpspers.com/image/390801620/?terms=Greater%Blondon%2Bnews%2Bstevens%2Band%2Bhazlettqq.

Chapter 4

1 The dialogue and examination and cross examination of the witness during the trial were constructed through various books, newspaper accounts, articles and brief mentions, and existing court documents found in online databases and professional threads. The language and roles were derived from traditional court proceedings and the assignments of everyone who appeared on the stand.

2 Villard, O. G., *John Brown, 1800–1859: A Biography Fifty Years After* (Washington, D.C.: Westphalia Press, 2016), p. 485.
3 *Ibid.*
4 *Ibid.*
5 "The Harpers Ferry Trials: the Conviction of Hazlett," *The Western Democrat,* vol. 8 #401, p. 2 (Charlotte, NC: W. J. & E. A. Yates, 1860)
6 *Ibid.*
7 *Ibid.*
8 Hinton, R., *John Brown and His Men*, p. 500.
9 Cress, J. D., "Cumberland County's Connection to John Brown's Raid at Harpers Ferry," *Cumberland County History*, vol. 26, p. 53.

Chapter 5

1 Cress, J. D., "Cumberland County's Connection to John Brown's Raid at Harpers Ferry," *Cumberland County History*, vol. 26, p. 48.
2 *Ibid.*
3 The pistol on display at the Kansas Historical Society is a .44 Colt revolver. It is a Percussion Lock 1st model Dragoon Revolver. The historical society states, "Part round, part octagonal, 7.5-inch barrel that is rifled with seven grooves. This revolver belonged to John Brown and was used by Albert G. Hazlett, one of Brown's men that aided in the raid on Harpers Ferry. Hazlett gave the revolver to Robert Smith who, in turn, passed it to his son Mathew A. Smith when Mathew enlisted at the start of the Civil War. Mathew then sold the gun to John M. Watson, who carried the gun for three years during the Civil War." (Retrieved from kansasmemory.org/item/324049.) Owen Brown's pistol at Chicago Museum is the same make and model.
4 Cress, *op. cit.*, p. 49.
5 *Ibid.*
6 *Ibid.*
7 *Ibid.*, p. 50.
8 *Ibid.*
9 *Ibid.*
10 *Ibid.*
11 *Ibid.*, p. 51.
12 *Ibid.*, p. 52.
13 *Ibid.*
14 *Ibid.*, p. 53.
15 *Ibid.*
16 *Ibid.*, p. 54.
17 *Ibid.*
18 This quote was from the website *A Day in the Life of the Civil War.* The article, "If I Had Ten Thousand Lives," was written by a blogger who calls herself LivingInVermont. It was posted on Sunday, March 16, 2014 at 4.42 a.m. The article was retrieved from lifeofthecivilwar.blogspot.com/2014/03/if-i-had-ten-thousand-lives.html.
19 Cress, *op. cit.*, p. 56.

Chapter 6

1 Anderson, O., *A Voice From Harpers Ferry: A Narrative of Events at Harpers Ferry*, (Boston: Printed for the Author, 1861), p. 51.
2 To contradict the narrative that Brown and his men did not find any willing slaves to take up arms (pikes that Brown contracted to have made for them), this segment out of Osborne's book serves as proof that some slaves did, indeed, fight for their own freedom, even though their pikes proved inferior to the guns of Lee's men. Freed black people helped in all phases of the plan. About fourteen or fifteen were at the schoolhouse to carry out various tasks. Others guarded prisoners. Some were transporters and messengers, while some actively recruited more black soldiers. This information can be found in a comprehensive article accessed through JSTOR. Geffert, H., (2002), "John Brown and His Black Allies: An Ignored Alliance," *The Pennsylvania Magazine of History and Biography*, 126(4), 591–610. Retrieved February 17, 2020, from jstor.org/stable/20093575
3 Lubet, S., *John Brown's Spy: The Adventurous Life and Tragic Confession of John E. Cook* (New Haven & London: Yale University Press, 2012), p. 110.
4 The quote comes from the website *Pennsylvania Civil War Trails* and the article entitled "Abolitionist John Brown Boards in Chambersburg." The site is a project of the Pennsylvania Tourism Office and no author credits are listed. It was accessed from pacivilwartrails.com/stories/tales/abolitionist-john-brown-boards-in-chambersburg
5 *Ibid.*
6 *Ibid.*
7 Lubet, *op. cit.*, p. 113.
8 *Ibid.*

Chapter 7

1 Anderson, O., *A Voice from Harpers Ferry: A Narrative of Events at Harpers Ferry*, (Boston: Printed for the Author, 1861), p. 28.
2 *Ibid.*, pp. 23–24.
3 *Ibid.*, pp. 28–29.
4 *Ibid.*, p. 31.
5 *Ibid.*, p. 32.
6 *History Net.com* posted an article by Steven Lubet entitled "Busted!: John E. Cook." The article was an adaptation from his book *John Brown's Spy: The Adventurous Life and Tragic Confession of John E. Cook* (Yale University Press, 2012). The article was originally published in the January 2013 issue of *America's Civil War.* It was accessed from historynet.com/busted-john-e-cook.html.
7 *Ibid.*
8 *Ibid*
9 Daigh, M., *John Brown in Memory and Myth* (Jefferson, NC: McFarland and Company, Inc., Publishers, 2015), p. 159.
10 Lubet, *John Brown's Spy.*
11 Hinton, R., *John Brown and His Men* p. 562.

12 *Ibid.*, p. 36.
13 *Ibid.*, p. 47.
14 *Ibid.*
15 *Ibid.*
16 *Ibid.*, p 49

17 *Ibid.*
18 Lubet, *op. cit.*
19 *Ibid.*
20 *Ibid.*
21 The quote comes from the "The Conspirators Biographies." The information in the article was said to be compiled from two sources: Connelley, W. E., *John Brown* (Topeka: Crane & Company, 1900), 340–347; and Villard, O. G., *John Brown, 1800–1859: A Biography Fifty Years After* (1910 reprint, Gloucester, MA: Peter Smith, 1965), 678–687. It reads, "I have also updated the language, and deleted some superfluous (in my opinion) information—ASR 3/21/95." Accessed from www2.iath.virginia.edu/jbrown/men.html.
22 Lubet, *op. cit.*
23 *Ibid.*
24 *Ibid.*
25 *Ibid.*
26 *Ibid.*

Chapter 8

1 "John Brown and James Montgomery," *The Linn County Clarion*, vol. XII, no. 26, p.1. Mound City, Linn County Kansas, July 15, 1887.
2 Clark, C., 'Augustus Wattles', *Kansas Bogus Legislature.org*, retrieved from kansasboguslegislature.org/free/wattles_a.html.
3 The article "119—The Kennedy Farm, circa 1852, south Washington County, MD" was found on the Washington County Historical Trust website. With no author credits, it is more of a promotional piece highlighting South Lynn and his preservation of the property. The article first appeared in *The Herald-Mail*, Sunday, September 12, 1999, as the 119th in the series. It was retrieved from washingtoncountyhistoricaltrust.org/the-kennedy-farm-circa-southern-washington-county-md/html.
4 *Ibid.*
5 Anderson, O., *A Voice from Harpers Ferry: A Narrative of Events at Harpers Ferry*, (Boston: Printed for the Author, 1861), p. 19.
6 Hearn, C. G., *Six Years of Hell: Harpers Ferry During the Civil War* (Baton Rouge: Louisiana State University Press, 1996), p. 11.
7 *Ibid.*
8 "More about the Hazlett Family," *The Indiana Weekly Messenger* (Indiana, PA, June 30, 1897).
9 *Ibid.*
10 Hearn, *op. cit.*, p. 10.
11 Brown, J. N., "Lovejoy's Influence on John Brown," *The Magazine of History with Notes and Queries*, vol. XXIII, nos. 3–4, p. 101, (Poughkeepsie, NY: William Abbatt), September–October 1916.
12 Chapin, L., "The Last Days of Old John Brown," *The Santa Cruz Daily Sentinel*, vol. XXX1, no. 7, p. 4 (Santa Cruz, CA: Saturday Morning, April 22, 1899). These quotes were taken from writings by Brown's oldest daughter, Ruth.

Though Ruth was an abolitionist, she refused to allow her husband, Henry Thompson, to take part in the raid. She was twenty-six at the time. Henry's two other brothers, William and Dauphin, joined the party, maybe out of loyalty to Brown or a sense of excitement. Many believed Dauphins motivation was to be closer to Annie at Kennedy Farm.

13 *Ibid.*
14 *Ibid.*
15 *Ibid.*
16 *Ibid.*
17 Eash, C., "'Into a Perfect Steel Trap'—Frederick Douglass and John Brown at Chambersburg," *Pennsylvania in the Civil War,* August 25, 2019. Retrieved from penncivilwar.com/post/into-a-perfect-steel-trap.html.
18 Hearn, *op. cit.*, p. 10.
19 Eash, *op. cit.*
20 *Ibid.*
21 *Ibid.*
22 DeCaro, L. A., Jr., "The Terrible Parable of Mrs. Huffmaster," *John Brown the Abolitionist—A Biographers Blog,* May 24, 2016. Retrieved from abolitionist-john-brown.blogspot.com/search?q=Huffmaster.
23 *Ibid.*
24 *Ibid.*
25 *Ibid.*
26 *Ibid.*
27 The source for these quotes come from a book entitle *Our Man in Charleston: Britian's Secret Agent in the Civil War South* written by Christopher Dickey. The book was published in New York by Broadway Books in 2015. On the website erenow.net, there was no page numbers, but Chapter 14 is the header where the quotes and strategies are found. Retrieved from erenow.net//ww/our-man-in-charleston-britains-secret-agent-in-the-civil-war-south/15.php.
28 Talbott, T., "John Brown's Hired Martial Help: Hugh Forbes," *Random Thoughts on History,* Petersburg, VA, November 8, 2009. Retrieved from randomthoughtshistory.blogspot.com/2009/11/john-browns-hired-martial-help-hugh.html.
29 *Ibid.*

Chapter 9

1 'More about the Hazlett Family', *The Indiana Weekly Messenger* (Indiana, PA, June 30, 1897).
2 Stewart, J. T., *Indiana County, Pennsylvania: Her People, Past, and Present, Embracing History of the County,* vol. 1 (Chicago: J.H. Beers & Co., 1913), p. 428.
3 Bower, C., 'History of Linn County', *Linn County Democrat* (Mound City, KS: February 9, 1911), vol. XXIII, no. 33, p. 1.
4 Kansas Historical Society, 'Proslavery Leader's Desk', *Kansapedia,* November 1998, modified December 2014. Retrieved from: https://www.kshs.org/kansapedia/proslavery-leader-s-desk/10309.
5 Holman, T. L., "James Montgomery in Kansas, 1854–1863" (1959), Electronic Thesis Collection, 125, digitalcommons.pittstate.edu/etd/125
6 *Ibid.*
7 Editors of the *Boston Traveller* [*sic.*], "Reminisces of Stephens [*sic.*] and Hazlett," *The Liberator* (Boston: J.B. Yerrinton & Sons, March 23, 1860) vol. 30, no. 12, p. 2.
8 Peterson, P. R., *Quantrill at Lawrence: The Untold Story* (Gretna, LA: Pelican Publishing Company, Inc., 2011), p. 105.
9 The article "Pottawatomie Massacre" is found on PBS.org. It is an adaptation from the film *John Brown's Holy War,* written by Ken Chowder and produced and directed by Robert Kenner. It was retrieved from pbs.org/wgbh/americanexperience/features/brown-pottawatomie-massacre/

10 The Summit County Historical Society of Akron Ohio runs a website with an article simply title "John Brown." In the article, Akron historian Carl Grismer believes that not only did these weapons come from Akron but cases of arms stored at the Summit County Jail made their way into Brown's hands. Retrieved from summithistory.org/john-brown.
11 Clark, C., 'Allen Wilkerson', *Kansas Bogus Legislature.org*, Retrieved from kansasboguslegislature.org/members/wilkinson_allen.html
12 *Ibid.*
13 *Ibid.*
14 *Ibid.*
15 *Ibid.*
16 *Ibid.*
17 *Ibid.*
18 *Ibid.*
19 *The Congressional Globe*, The Official Proceedings of Congress, Published by John C. Rives, Washington, D. C., Thirty-Sixth Congress, 1st Session, New Series, No. 7, Tuesday, December 13, 1859, pp. 105–106.
20 "The Pottawatomie Killings: It is Established Beyond Controversy That John Brown Was the Leader, Statement of James Townsley. 'Republican Citizen,'" Paola, Kansas, 20 Dec 1879, page 5, column 5. Retrieved from olatheschools.libguides.com/JohnBrown/PottawatomieKillings
21 *Ibid.*
22 "Pottawatomie Massacre," Retrieved from pbs.org/wgbh/americanexperience/features/brown-pottawatomie-massacre/
23 "Marais des Cygnes Massacre," *Civil War on the Western Border: the Missouri-Kansas Conflict 1854–1865*. This project is supported by the Institute of Museum and Library Services under the provisions of the Library Services and Technology Act as administered by the Missouri State Library, a division of the Office of the Secretary of State with additional support from the William T. Kemper Foundation - Commerce Bank, Trustee. The article was retrieved from civilwaronthewesternborder.org/timeline/marais-des-cygnes-massacre
24 "Remembering the Marais des Cygnes Massacre," *The Fort Scott Tribune,* March 3, 2008. Retrieved from fstribune.com/story/1315443.html
25 *Ibid.*
26 *Ibid.*
27 *Ibid.*
28 Reynolds, D.S., *John Brown, Abolitionist: The Man Who Killed Slavery, Sparked the Civil War, and Seeded Civil Rights The Man Who Killed Slavery, Sparked the Civil War, and Seeded Civil Rights* (New York: Vintage Books, 2006) p. 276.
29 The Federal Writer's Project, "Fort Scott," The WPA Guide to Kansas: The Sunflower State (San Antonio, TX: Trinity University Press, 2013), Retrieved from books.google.com/books?id=0VzpCAAAQBAJ&pg=PT157&source=gbs_toc_r&cad=3#v=onepage&q&f=false
30 Villard, O., *John Brown 1800–1859: A Biography Fifty Years After* (1910, reprint, Gloucester, MA: Peter Smith, 1965), p. 367.
31 Stoneham, M., *John Brown and the Era of Literary Confrontation* (Routledge, 2009), Retrieved from books.google.com/books?id=j0ZnDwAAQBAJ&source=gbs_navlinks_s
32 Villard, *op. cit.*, p. 368.
33 *Ibid.*
34 Patrick Brophy wrote a book entitled *Three Hundred Years*, published by D. G. L.

InfoWrite in 1993. There is an excerpt of the author's account on the Spring Grove Monthly Meeting website. The article was retrieved from sgmm.org/plainandsimple/brophys.

35 *Ibid.*
36 Villard, *op. cit.* pp 369–370.
37 *Ibid.*
38 Brophy, P., sgmm.org/plainandsimple/brophys.html.
39 *Ibid.*
40 Wilson, H.P., *John Brown, Soldier of Fortune* (Cedar Rapids, Iowa: The Torch Press, 1913), p. 270.
41 *Ibid.*
42 Brophy, P., sgmm.org/plainandsimple/brophys.html.
43 *Ibid.*
44 *Ibid.*
45 *Ibid.*
46 "John Brown's Army: The Man from Indiana County," The Historical and Genealogical Society of Indiana County Blog.

Bibliography

"119—The Kennedy Farm, *circa* 1852, South Washington County, MD." *Washington County Historical Trust*, washingtoncountyhistoricaltrust.org/the-kennedy-farm-circa-1852-southern-washington-county-md/.

"Abolitionist John Brown Boards in Chambersburg." *Abolitionist John Brown Boards in Chambersburg | Pennsylvania Civil War Trails*, The Pennsylvania Tourism Office, pacivilwartrails.com/stories/tales/abolitionist-john-brown-boards-in-chambersburg.

Anderson, O., "A Voice from Harper's Ferry: Osborne P. Anderson (1861)." *A Voice from Harper's Ferry | Osborne P. Anderson (1861)*, 1861, historyisaweapon.com/defcon1/andersonvoiceharpersferry.html.

Barrett, T., *Harpers Ferry: the Story of John Brown's Raid* (Millbrook Press, 1993), accessed from *Google Books*, books.google.com/books/about/Harpers_Ferry.html?id=euET3HvuM1oC.

Barry, J., *Strange Story of Harper's Ferry: with Legends of the Surrounding Country (Classic Reprint)* (FORGOTTEN Books, 2015)

Bourgeois, M. G., *All Things Human: the Social Gospel of Henry Codman Potter, 1834–1908*. jstor.org/stable/10.5406/j.ctt1xckjd ed., Urbana and Chicago, 2004.

Bridgeford-Smith, J., "Money, Morality and Madness." *America's Civil War*, vol. 28, no. 4, Sept. 2015, p. 46. EBSCOhost, search.ebscohost.com/login.aspx?direct=true&db=f6h&AN=103267901&site=ehost-live.

Brophy, P., "John Brown, and 'Sam and Jane' on the Underground Railroad." *Exploring the Underground Railroad* (Montgomery and Bridget Fitzwater, 2002), sgmm.org/plainandsimple/firsttrip.html#Brophy.

Brophy, P., *Three Hundred Years: Historical Highlights of Nevada and Vernon County, Missouri* (D.G. Logan, DGL Info Write, 1993)

Brown, J. N., "HathiTrust Digital Library." *The Magazine of History with Notes and Queries*, XXIII, no. 3-4, September–October 1916. babel.hathitrust.org/cgi/pt?id=hvd.32044090111956&view=1up&seq=126&q1=john%20brown

Chan, A., "Busted!: John E. Cook." *HistoryNet*, 10 July 2017, historynet.com/busted-john-e-cook.htm.

Chapin, L. V., "The Last Days of Old John Brown," *The Santa Cruz Dailey Sentinel*, April 22, 1899, newspapers.com/image/?clipping_id=7260973&fcfToken=eyJhbGciOiJIUzI1NiIsInR5cCI6IkpXVCJ9.eyJmcmVlLXZpZXctaWQiOjUyNTYxMjM2LCJpYXQiOjE1OTY3MjMyNDMsImV4cCI6MTU5NjgwOTY0M30.8nqRsNxhTlUOptLLlBOXbmXMo65zl9pux_-Z0oAieQs.

Clark, C., "Allen Wilkinson," *Kansas Bogus Legislature*, kansasboguslegislature.org/.

Clark, C., "Augustus Wattles," *Kansas Bogus Legislature*, kansasboguslegislature.org/.

Connelley, W. E., *John Brown* (FORGOTTEN Books, 2016)

The Congressional Globe, 36th Congress, 12 December 1859, pp. 105–106. *The Library of Congress*, memory.loc.gov/cgibin/ampage?collId=llcg&fileName=051/llcg051.db&recNum=183

Cress, Joseph D. "Cumberland County's Connection to John Brown's Raid at Harpers Ferry." *Cumberland County History*, vol. 26, 2009, gardnerlibrary.org/sites/default/files/vol26n1.pdf#page=26.

Daigh, M., *John Brown in Memory and Myth* (McFarland & Company, Inc., Publishers, 2015)

Daniel, A. M., "Quotes from John Brown." *Negro History Bulletin*, vol. 30, no. 5, 1967, pp. 6–7. JSTOR, jstor.org/stable/24766458.

DeCaro, L. A., "A Biographer's Blog," *John Brown the Abolitionist*, January 1, 1970, abolitionist-john-brown.blogspot.com/2015/09/the-second-harpers-ferry-raid-fate-of.html.

DeCaro, L., *John Brown: the Cost of Freedom* (International Publishers, 2007)

Dickey, C., Our Man in Charleston: Britain›s Secret Agent in the Civil War South United States (Crown, 2015)

Dirck, B. R., "By the Hand of God: James Montgomery and Redemptive Violence" *Kansas History: A Journal of the Central Plains*, vol. 27, 2004, pp. 100–115., kshs.org/publicat/history/2004spring_dirck.pdf.

Dixon, M. E., "The Surprising Role One Local Man Played in the Deadly Harpers Ferry Raid." *Main Line Today*, December 1, 2019, mainlinetoday.com/life-style/the-surprising-role-one-local-man-played-in-the-deadly-harpers-ferry-raid/.

Eash, C., "Frederick Douglass and John Brown at Chambersburg, 1859." *PA in the Civil War*, August 25, 2019, penncivilwar.com/post/into-a-perfect-steel-trap.

Editors of *The Traveller*. "Reminiscences of Stephens and Hazlett." *The Liberator, Newspapers.Com*, March 23, 1860.

Erdelac, E. M., "Albert Hazlett." *Delirium Tremens*, July 4, 2016, 10.58 a.m., emerdelac.wordpress.com/tag/albert-hazlett/.

Featherstonhaugh, T., *John Brown's Men: the Lives of Those Killed at Harper's Ferry, with a Supplementary Bibliography of John Brown* (Harrisburg Pub. Co., 1899)

Featherstonhaugh, T., "The Final Burial of the Followers of John Brown," New *England Magazine*, 1901, wvculture.org/history/jbexhibit/bbspr03-0015.html.

Federal Writers' Project, *The WPA Guide to Kansas: The Sunflower State* (United States, Trinity University Press, 2013), accessed from *Google Books*, google.com/books/edition/The_WPA_Guide_to_Kansas/0VzpCAAAQBAJ?hl=en&gbpv=0

Editorial Staff, "Remembering the Marais Des Cygnes Massacre." *Fort Scott Tribune*, March 3, 2008, fstribune.com/story/1315443.html.

Szemcsak. F. and B., *Slave Owners, Abolitionists Lived in Perth Amboy*, January 1, 1970, historicperthamboy.blogspot.com/2011/12/slave-owners-abolitionists-lived-in.html?showComment=1551371985284#c8349115315101700013.

Fuller, D., "Thoreau and John Brown's Pottawatomie." *The Thoreau Society Bulletin*, no. 210, 1995, pp. 2–3. JSTOR, jstor.org/stable/23400726.

Geffert, H. N., "John Brown and His Black Allies: An Ignored Alliance." *The Pennsylvania Magazine of History and Biography*, vol. 126, no. 4, 2002, pp. 591–610. JSTOR, jstor.org/stable/20093575.

Gilpin, R. B., *John Brown Still Lives!: America's Long Reckoning with Violence, Equality, and Change*. The University of North Carolina Press, 2011. EBSCOhost, search.ebscohost.com/login.aspx?direct=true&db=nlebk&AN=365274&site=ehost-live.

Gobrecht, L. E., "National Historic Landmark Nomination." NPG Gallery, United States Department of Interior, National Park Service, November 21, 1997, npgallery.nps.gov/GetAsset/07aed8c1-26c4-4d8c-80ca-48c6f280c35a/.

Green, M. and Johnston, K. G., "Joshua Young," Unitarian Universalist History & Heritage Society (UUHHS), August 8, 2018, uudb.org/articles/joshuayoung.html.

"Harpers Ferry Revolver," *Kansas Historical Society*, January 2009, kshs.org/kansapedia/harpers-ferry-revolver/10248.

Hearn, C. G., *Six Years of Hell: Harpers Ferry during the Civil War* (Louisiana State University Press, 1999)

HGSIC, Author. "Absalom Hazlett: Abolitionist from Indiana County," *HGSIC Historical Happenings*, Historical and Genealogical Society of Indiana County, September 27, 2017, hgsic.wordpress.com/2016/03/15/absalom-hazlett-abolitionist-from-indiana-county/.

Hinton, R., "John Brown and His Men: Richard J. Hinton": Free Download, Borrow, and Streaming." *Internet Archive*, University of Michigan, January 22, 2015, archive.org/details/bub_gb_A3xqoeRmh_sC/page/n519/mode/2up?q=albert%2Bhazlett.

Hinton, R., *John Brown and His Men: With Some Account of the Roads They Traveled to Reach Harper's Ferry* by Richard Josiah Hinton—Revised Edition—1894, Books on Google Play." Google, February 2, 2010, play.google.com/store/books/details?id=uiaYWp66b-cC&rdid=book-uiaYWp66b-cC&rdot=1.

Holman, T. L., "James Montgomery in Kansas, 1854-1863" (1959). Electronic Thesis Collection. 125. digitalcommons.pittstate.edu/etd/125

Horwitz, T., "Why John Brown Still Scares Us," *American History*, vol. 46, no. 5, Dec. 2011, p. 38. EBSCOhost, search.ebscohost.com/login.aspx?direct=true&db=f6h&AN=66520584&site=ehost-live.

Hunt, H., "Absalom (Albert) Hazlett Historical Marker Dedication," *Flickr*, Yahoo!, April 1, 2009, flickr.com/photos/harry_hunt/3405450490/in/photostream/.

"John Brown and His Men," *The Sun*, September 2, 1899, newspapers.com/image/207079063/?terms=absalom hazlett.

"The John Brown Farm," *Negro History Bulletin*, vol. 22, no. 7, 1959, pp. 152–152. JSTOR, jstor.org/stable/44215528.

"John Brown House." *FCHS*, Franklin County Historical Society, 2019, franklinhistorical.org/john-brown-house.

"The John Brown Letters (Concluded)," *The Virginia Magazine of History and Biography*, vol. 11, no. 1, 1903, pp. 26–32. JSTOR, jstor.org/stable/4242570. Accessed August 5, 2020.

"John Brown's Raid," John Brown's Raid, August 2017, p. 1. EBSCOhost, search.ebscohost.com/login.aspx?direct=true&db=f6h&AN=21212439&site=ehost-live.

Johnson, M., "An 'Ever Present Bone of Contention': The Heyward Shepherd Memorial," *West Virginia History Journal*, 56 (1997), 1–26.

Keller, A., *Thunder at Harper's Ferry* (Englewood Cliffs, N. J.: Prentice-Hall, 1958)

Kolander, F. G., "Absalom (Albert) H. Hazlett." geni_family_tree, November 17, 2014, geni.com/people/Absalom-Albert-Hazlett/6000000001768584187.

Lieberth, D., "Perkins & Brown Partnership." *Perkins & Brown Partnership | The Summit County Historical Society of Akron Ohio*, Summit County Historical Society, 2020, summithistory.org/perkins-brown-partnership.

LivingInVermont, *A Day in the Life of the Civil War*, January 1, 1970, lifeofthecivilwar.blogspot.com/.

Lubet, S., *John Brown's Spy: The Adventurous Life and Tragic Confession of John E Cook* (Yale University Press, 2014), accessed from *Google Books*, books.google.com/books?id=TD49f2F0DP8C.

Lynn, S. T., "Kennedy Farm National Historic Landmark: Facebook," Facebook, January 5, 2012, facebook.com/groups/255083434558258.

Lynn, S. and Gardner, D., "John Brown's Cabin (Kennedy Farm)." John Brown's Cabin/Facebook, November 5, 2010, facebook.com/John-Browns-cabin-Kennedy-Farm-143270022387489.

McGlone, R. E., "The 'Madness' of John Brown." *Civil War Times*, vol. 48, no. 5, October 2009, p. 42. EBSCOhost, search.ebscohost.com/login.aspx?direct=true&db=f6h&AN=43815772&site=ehost-live.

McTaggart, U., "Historical Fiction about John Brown and Male Identity in Radical Movements." *African American Review*, vol. 51, no. 2, Summer 2018, p. 129. EBSCOhost, doi:10.1353/afa.2018.0019.

Meyer, E. L. "Sole Survivor." *The Washington Post*, WP Company, December 12, 2004, washingtonpost.com/archive/lifestyle/magazine/2004/12/12/sole-survivor/650ade08-8488-4959-bb29-8cd98e1644c6/.

"More About the Harpers Ferry Difficulty," *Cincinnati Daily Press*, October 31, 1859, newspapers.com/image/70794602/?terms=more%2Babout%2Bthe%2Bharpers%2Bferry%2Bdifficulty.

"More About the Hazlett Family," *The Indiana Weekly Messenger*, June 30, 1897, newspapers.com/image/13957863/?terms=absalom hazlett.

Nasby, D., *Harpers Ferry* (Arcadia Pub., 2007)

Oates, S. B., *To Purge this Land with Blood: A Biography of John Brown* (New York: Harper & Row, 1970)

Petersen, P. R., *Quantrill at Lawrence: The Untold Story* (Pelican Pub. Co., 2011)

Phillips, C., "October 16,1859: John Brown Raids Harpers Ferry." *American History*, vol. 40, no. 4, Oct. 2005, p. 16. EBSCOhost, search.ebscohost.com/login.aspx?direct=true&db=f6h&AN=17843929&site=ehost-live.

"Pottawatomie Massacre." *PBS, Public Broadcasting Service*, 2000, pbs.org/wgbh/americanexperience/features/brown-pottawatomie-massacre/.

"Proslavery Leader's Desk." *Kansas Historical Society*, November 1998, kshs.org/kansapedia/proslavery-leader-s-desk/10309#:~:text=This%20desk%20was%20brought%20to,on%20the%20issue%20of%20slavery.

Ranieri, J. M., "The Graveside." *John Brown Farm Cemetery—North Elba, Essex County, New York*, nnytombstoneproject.net/essex/north_elba/john_brown.htm.

Rein, C., "'Marais des Cygnes Massacre' Civil War on the Western Border: The Missouri-Kansas Conflict, 1854–1865" (The Kansas City Public Library), civilwaronthewesternborder.org/encyclopedia/marais-des-cygnes-ma...

Renehan, E. J., Jr., *The Secret Six: The True Tale of the Men Who Conspired with John Brown* (Columbia: University of South Carolina Press, 1997)

Reynolds, D. S., *John Brown, Abolitionist: the Man Who Killed Slavery, Sparked the Civil War, and Seeded Civil Rights* (Vintage Books, 2006)

Rowland, T., "John Brown's Moonlight March," *America's Civil War*, vol. 22, no. 4, September 2009, p. 29. EBSCOhost, search.ebscohost.com/login.aspx?direct=true&db=f6h&AN=43169888&site=ehost-live.

Sanborn, F. B., *The Life and Letters of John Brown* (Boston: Roberts Brothers, 1891)

Shackel, P. A., "Terrible Saint: Changing Meanings of the John Brown Fort." *Historical Archaeology*, vol. 29, no. 4, 1995, pp. 11–25. JSTOR, jstor.org/stable/25616421. Accessed August 5, 2020.

Siebert, W. H. and Hart, A. B., *The Underground Railroad from Slavery to Freedom: a Comprehensive History* (Dover Publications Inc., 2006)

Spring, R., Stanford University Department of Special Collections, M0541, Rebecca Spring Papers, box X, folder Y.

Stephenson, C. D., *Indiana County 175th Anniversary History* (A.G. Halldin Pub. Co., 1978)

Stephenson, C. D. *The Impact of the Slavery Issue on Indiana County* (Mahoning Mimeograph & Pamphlet Service, 1964)

Stephenson, C., "A Harpers Ferry Insurectionist [*sic.*]," *Indiana Gazette*, July 3, 1976, newspapers.com/image/14050154/?terms=absalom hazlett.

Stephenson, C., "Six Indiana Countians Serve in Congress," *Indiana Gazette*, January 21, 1984, newspapers.com/image/519406698/?terms=absalom hazlett.

Stoneham, M., *John Brown and the Era of Literary Confrontation* (United Kingdom, Taylor & Francis, 2009), accessed from Google Books, google.com/books/edition/John_Brown_and_the_Era_of_Literary_Confr/j0ZnDwAAQBAJ?hl=en&gbpv=0

Stewart, J. T., *Indiana County, Pennsylvania: Her People, Past and Present, Embracing a History of the County and a Biographical Record of Representative Families* (J.H. Beers & Co., 1913), accessed from Google Books, play.google.com/store/books/details?id=fM0wAQAAMAAJ&rdid=book-fM0wAQAAMAAJ&rdot=1.

Townsley, J., "Pottawatomie Massacre, 1856: John Brown History: Kansas History," *Pottawatomie Massacre, 1856 | John Brown History | Kansas History*, ["Republican Citizen," Paola, Kansas, 20 Dec 1879, Page 5, Column 5], March 8, 2017, kansashistory.us/pottamassacre.html.

Truby, J., *The Anatomy of Story: 22 Steps to Becoming a Master Storyteller* (Faber and Faber, 2008)

United States, Congress, Cong. Senate, The Select Committee of the Senate, and James M. Mason. *Invasion at Harpers Ferry*, 36AD. 36th Congress, 1st session, report 278. *Senate.gov*, HarpersFerryInvestigation1860.pdf.

Utter, D. N., "John Brown of Osawatomie." *The North American Review*, vol. 137, no. 324, 1883, pp. 435–446. JSTOR, jstor.org/stable/25118327.

Villard, O. G., *John Brown, 1800–1859: A Biography Fifty Years after (1910 Classic Reprint)* (FORGOTTEN Books, 2015)

White, D. J., "Antislavery Violence and Secession, October 1859–April 1861," University of Alabama, 2017, ir.ua.edu/bitstream/handle/123456789/3438/file_1.pdf?sequence=1&isAllowed=y.

"Whitelaw Reid on the Independent Press." *The Goodland Republic and Goodland News*, 13 Oct. 1899, p. 4. newspapers.com/clip/8847376/intellectual-prostitutes-quote-whitelaw/.

Wired Studios, "Albert Hazlett—Trial in Carlisle, October 1859." *Blog Divided "Post Topic" Albert Hazlett—Trial in Carlisle, October 1859* (Dickinson College, 2016), housedivided.dickinson.edu/sites/blogdivided/2010/07/02/albert-hazlett-trial-in-carlisle-october-1859/.

Wilson, H. P., *John Brown, Soldier of Fortune—A Critique—The Original Classic Edition* (Emereo Publishing., 1913)

Wolfe, H. S., "A Biographer's Blog." *John Brown the Abolitionist*, Louis DeCaro, January 1, 1970, abolitionist-john-brown.blogspot.com/2015/08/the-second-harpers-ferry-raid-fate-of.html?m=1.